REMEDIAL VAASTU
for
Homes

REMEDIAL VAASTU
for
Homes

Dr. N.H. Sahasrabuddhe
M.E. (I.I.Sc.) F.I.V. Ph.D

and

Janhavi N. Sahasrabuddhe
M.S.E. (Computer Networks)
University of Pennsylvania
B.E. (E & TC) Pune University

STERLING☰

STERLING PUBLISHERS (P) LTD.
Regd. Office: A1/256 Safdarjung Enclave,
New Delhi-110029. CIN: U22110DL1964PTC211907
Phone: +91 82877 98380
e-mail: mail@sterlingpublishers.in
www.sterlingpublishers.in

Remedial Vaastu for Homes
© 2019, Dr. N. H. Sahasrabuddhe & Janhavi N. Sahasrabuddhe
978 81 207 7319 6
First Edition - 2012
Reprint - 2015, 2019, 2020, 2021, 2023

Printed in India

Printed and Published by Sterling Publishers Pvt. Ltd.,
Plot No. 13, Ecotech-III, Greater Noida-201306, U.P., India

With love and respect
we dedicate this book to

Guruji Sri Sri Ravishankar

Founder,

Art of Living Foundation

and

Ved Vignan Maha Vidyapeeth

whose presence inspires and guides us in life.

Preface

Darshanshastra is the starting point for understanding the significance of any of the ancient Indian sciences. The extensively studied disciplines like Yogashastra, Jyotishshastra, Vaastushastra, Aayurveda and Sangeet have their origins in Darshanshastra. Rather, these disciplines are known as 'Upangas' (sub-branches) of Darshanshastra. It is interesting to note that all these sub-branches follow a common logical pattern for analysing and understanding a given situation. Astrology studies the effect of planetary positions and directions on an individual, while Vaastushastra studies the impact on Vaastu, of cosmic forces with all their directional aspects. In all these disciplines, a Vaastu is assumed to be a living soul having close affinity with the individual dwelling in it.

Dr.N.H.Sahasrabuddhe
Janhavi N. Sahasrabuddhe

"Venkatesh Villa", 1st Floor,
1202/2A/1, Apte Road,
Behind Hotel Surya, Pune-411005.
e-mail: dr.nhs.vaastu@gmail.com
           janhavi.sahasrabuddhe@gmail.com
Tel.: (Off.) 020-25531989, 65006487
Mob.: 09822011050

Contents

Vaastushastra – Theory and Practice

Life, though beyond logic, is certainly not illogical. Life descends from immensity that is an ocean of logic. But this immensity itself is infinitely far away from man's comprehension that makes him wonder whether life is beyond logic.

Minute human thoughts cannot find cosmic link. Holistic existence can create contradictions with logic, the all-encompassing source of life. Traditional science reflects this fundamental truth through the comprehensive perception of nature. Perception begins where the confines of cause and effect end. Traditional medical disciplines lead to *Kaya Kalpa* (transformation of body), Yogashastra results in *Mana Kalpa* (transformation of mind) and Vaastushastra shows the way to *Bhagya Kalpa* (transformation of fortunes).

Water, wind, light, stones, metals, plants, herbs, pyramids, crystals, colours, helix, mystic curves serve as catalysts in Vaastushastra for rectifying the cosmic alignment of an individual. Changes brought about in the holistic existence of man by these remedies guide him to positive relationships, satisfaction in all his endeavours, happiness, bliss and grace.

Enhancing the benign moon streams (*Ida*) and curtailing the devastating sun streams (*Pingala*) are the foundations of Vaastushastra. The core Vaastushastra revolves around addition, subtraction, manipulation and reworking of virtues and vices of human beings and nature. The divine knowledge of Vaastu can provide cosmic envelope to human beings at all levels of existence.

Jyotisha (astrology) and Yogashastra are prerequisites for learning Vaastushastra. Cosmos is divided into 27 parts known as constellations. These constellations are classified on the basis of five great elements and planets. The virtues and vices of the five great elements are reflected in certain earthly entities like plants, colours, metals and gems that are under the influence of constellations. The relationship of directions with plants, colours, metals and stones gives great variety and multiple dimensions to Vaastu remedial measures. A new momentum is imparted to cosmic rhythm, directional frequencies, and natural synchronies through these corrective actions. An individual is then freed of his old reference and sets foot in fresh reality. Vastushstra blesses him with a new direction in life, fresh span, and a unique axis of reference.

Yogashastra deals with inner spaces of human beings. Spaces with *Satwa-Guna* are full of Prana, spaces with *Rajo-Guna* are filled with self-ego, and spaces with *Tamo-Guna* are nothing but voids in life. Yogic processes refill all these spaces with Prana and eliminate the voids in the macrocosm of primordial sounds. Vaastushastra in co-ordination with astrology and Yogashastra can provide a holistic cure for all the problems in the world.

While constructing a house, the divine Vaastu knowledge acts on the qualities of an individual and the cosmos, as Vaastushastra is the cosmic bridge between microcosm (the inner spaces) and macrocosm (the outer spaces).

Vibrations, waves, sound and light are the four basic instruments of Vaastushastra. Examples are aplenty to indicate that a right blending of these parameters leads to positivity, while a wrong combination leads to negativity.

For ages, astrology has been used for understanding and predicting an individual's destiny. Astrology has also been extensively referred to pinpointing the set of mind and body of a person, including any diseases, infections and handicaps. Since Vaastushastra treats any Vaastu as a living soul, it is not difficult to understand the relevance of astrology, which defines the positions of planets in specific directions, while Vaastushastra analysis has Vaastu-Directions as the operating factor. Thus, a common platform for both these disciplines is easily established.

After an extensive study of hundreds of dwellings, horoscopes of the owners of these houses, their living conditions, their careers, their family backgrounds, etc. it was evident that the horoscopes of the occupants of Vaastu could pinpoint the *Vaastudosha* of their dwellings. Deciding the effective remedial measure against *Vaastudosha* on the basis of the horoscope and the vaastu-pursh-mandal was the next logical step. During this exercise, it became clear that the matching of astrology and Vaastushastra was flawless, whether it was Vaastu-situation or the remedial measures.

While Jyotisha gives insight into *Vaastudosha* and general remedial action, Yogashastra shows the path towards building a proactive shield against effects of directional deficiencies. Modern science can serve its purpose by providing an analytical approach and efficient techniques in implementing Vaastu principles. Vaastushastra enquiry must involve a multidisciplinary and multidimensional approach for guiding the human mind that has lost its way in the confusing scenario of the modern era.

1

Introduction

Vaastushastra is an age-old science. First reference to it could be traced around ten thousand years back. Great ascetic maharshis like Bhrugu, Atri and Vasishtha are the founders of this science. In Jain philosophy many *aagams* are devoted to this science. Origin of Vaastushastra can be understood by understanding the cosmic form called *Shivlingakruti*. This cosmic symbol showers peace, prosperity and bliss, that is, *Satyam, Shivam, Sundaram*. As a matter of form and as a matter of energy, it completely follows the tenets of Vaastushastra. Elements of Vaastushastra are related to 8 directions, 5 great elements and energy streams. Every human being is comprised of the 5 great elements. Nature is also controlled by the same 5 great elements; hence, if a house can cultivate a positive relationship between human beings and nature then it's a perfect home. The rules of Vaastushastra regulate the relationship between nature and individual by regulating the personal and cosmic breath.

Shivlingakruti

Purpose, person and form is the perfect projection of Vaastushastra which can be learnt through the perfect form of Shivlingakruti. Where there is balance of energy and matter, there lies beauty of existence and light. In traditional language it is called '*Shivshakti Samagam*'. A perfect form which is attuned to the characters of directions naturally

SOUTH OR WEST

HIGH
HEAVY
LESS

NORTH OR EAST

LOW
LIGHT
MORE

leads to peace, prosperity and progress. The complete concept of Vaastushastra can be understood through the *Shivlingakruti* form, where matter explodes into dynamic energy and forces its travel in the *mandalakar* path.

The Concept of 5 Great Elements

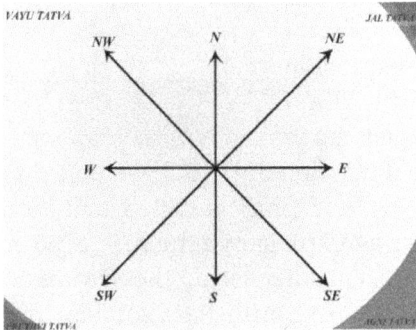

2.1 Water (Jal Tatwa)

It is a divine element which has profound power to purify anything on earth. When light falls on water it becomes a divine flame. North and water together give success and wealth. North-East and water together give divinity and sacredness. Water

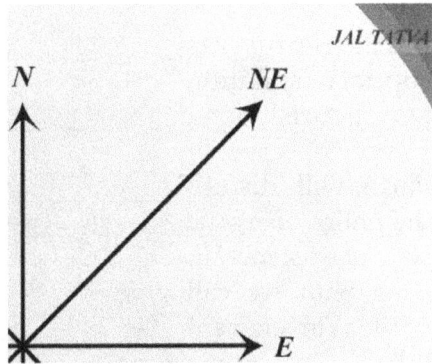

surface acts like a super crystal. Hence, water symbolises Moon, North, crystal, silver pearl and white marble.

2.2 Fire *(Agni Tatwa)*

Fire is defined as a reflection of intelligence, ego, lust and warmth. Where there is right expression of fire, divine flame emerges and motherly warmth follows. Where there is wrong expression of fire, there is explosion and irritation. East and South-East both represent the Fire element. In East zone it is a positive flame which in Feng Shui is called Chi. South-East zone represents fire as explosion which is a wrong version of fire. Hence, in Vaastushastra, the expression of East is enhanced and that of South-East zone is controlled by the divine element of Fire.

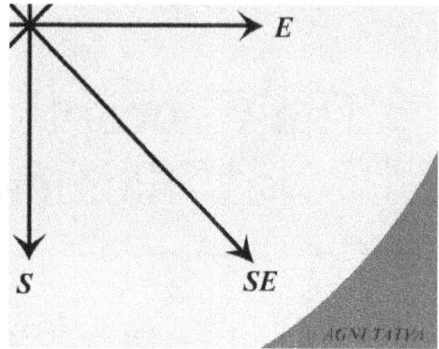

2.3 Earth *(Prithvi Tatwa)*

Earth represents support, stability, and nourishment. Hence, absence of Earth will disturb the entire energetic state of existence. In Feng Shui we call it the Yin element which remains passive and gives more space to the Yang effects. Excessive Earth element in the source zones kills positive energy in the house, leading to death, destruction, discontinuity and defamation. South-

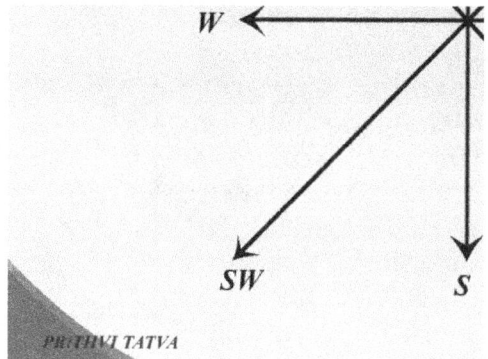

West zone represents this element and is termed as the main Sink direction.

2.4 Wind *(Vaayu Tatwa)*

Wind represents *Prana,* wind represents activity, wind represents mind, too.

VAYU TATVA

NW

N

W

Where there is right expression of Wind, there one finds rhythm and synchronicity, which can be equated with the cooling breeze. Where there is Katrina and Rita, there lies a wrong version of Wind element, which obviously leads to all types of disturbances in the individual as well as the world.

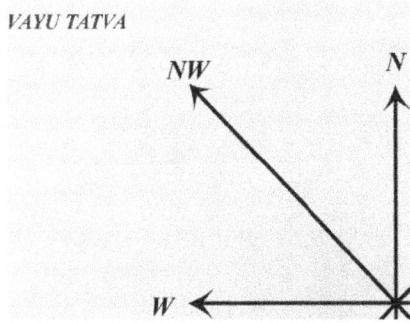

2.5 Ether *(Akash Tatwa)*

Where there is no space, there lies void; void means content is totally missing. Where there is Space there lies love, happiness and breathing of all virtues. Rather, Vaastushastra is the science of space. Space represents interrelationship of all elements, interrelationships

Akash Tatwa

N

S

E

between human beings. Definition of Space is Void + Energy. Streaming of energy, using the principles of Vaastushastra, removes the voids and rehabilitates human beings.

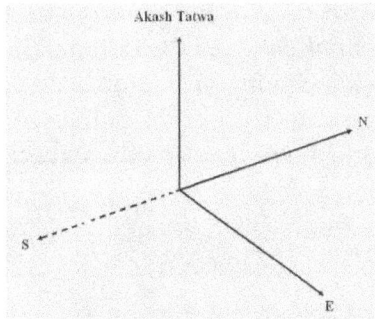

2.6 Source and Sink Energy

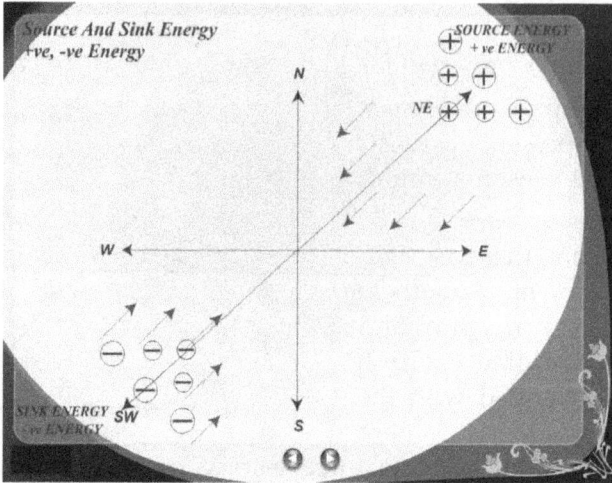

Source And Sink Energy
+ve, -ve Energy

SOURCE ENERGY
+ ve ENERGY

SINK ENERGY
-ve ENERGY

It is obvious that N, NE and E are Source directions of energy whereas S, SW and W are Sink directions. North is the source direction of 'organic streams', whereas South is the sink direction of 'organic streams'. East is the source direction of *pranik energy* and West is the sink direction of *pranik energy*. In traditional language we call it *urja*. Hence, connection with North and East leads to experience of resourceful events in life whereas relationship with South and West leads to the experience of sinking events in life.

3

Slopes and Gradients in Vaastu

Slopes towards source directions, i.e. N, NE, E are resourceful, and slopes towards sink directions, i.e. S, SW and W are harmful.

Following effects can be observed as per the slope of the plot:

3.1 If land is sloping towards East

It showers prosperity, intelligence, male progeny and all types of skills.

3.2 If land is sloping towards South-East

It is the first sink direction which leads to fire hazards, quarrels, fights and female progeny.

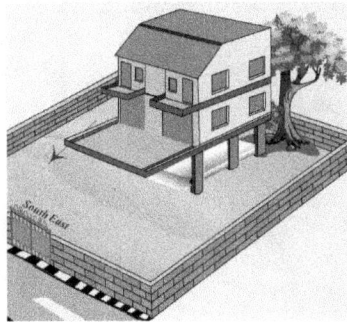

3.3 If land is sloping towards South

It leads to death, destruction and defamation.

3.4 If land is sloping towards South-West

It leads to accidents, murders and suicides.

3.5 If land is sloping towards West

It leads to divorce, defamation and disagreement in every walk of life.

3.6 If land is sloping towards North-West

It leads to prosperity, activity and advertisement. This is the first source direction.

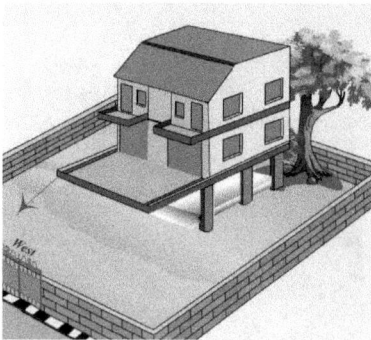

3.7 If land is sloping towards North

It leads to peace, prosperity and progress.

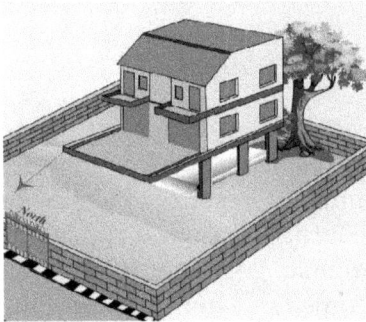

3.8 If land is sloping towards North-East

It leads to the experience of completeness in life since North-East is the most divine direction amongst all the directions.

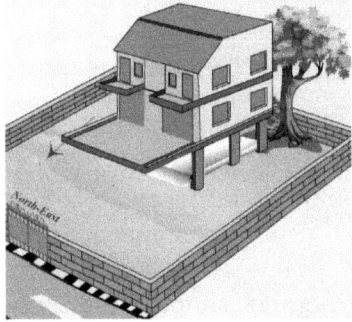

4

Irregular Shapes in Vaastu

Corner Extensions and Cut of Plots

Where there is square or rectangular geometry, there emerges the quality of Earth element, which showers stability, support and nourishment. A perfect balance of all aspirations and a correct contribution of all directions happens in a square or rectangular geometry. Hence, all irregular shapes and non-geometric extensions or cuts disturb the balance of the house, which in turn creates the imbalance of the 5 great elements, and the aspirations of all the directions do not contribute in a simple symmetric way.

4.1 Extensions and cuts in SE zone
It disturbs the Fire element leading to infertility in women, childless couples, fire hazards, anger and violence.

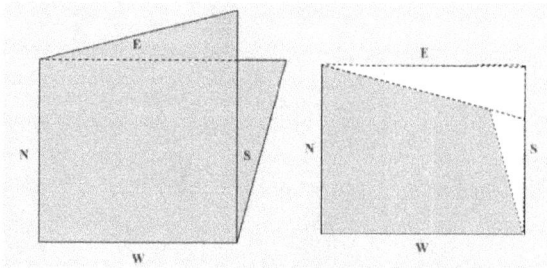

Remedies for this type of plot:

1) Bury pearls at four places in the extended South-East zone.

2) Bury 35gm silver in the South-East zone.

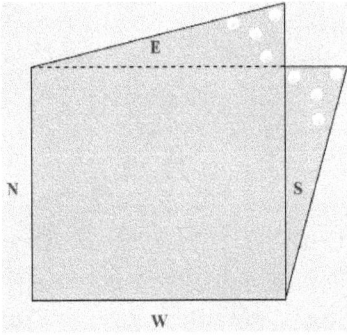

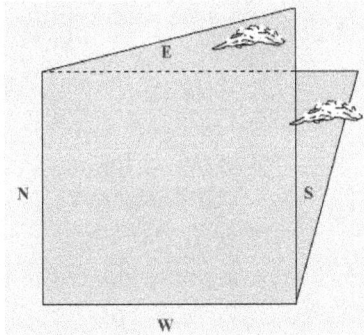

3) Use white marble in the extended South-East zone.

4) Use almond and christmas plants in the extended South-East area.

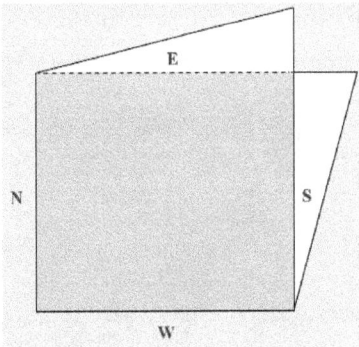

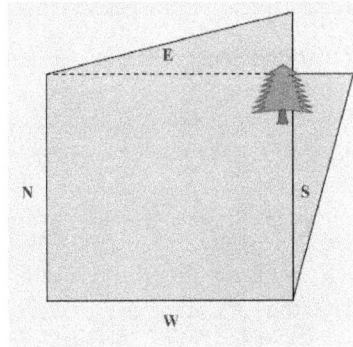

5) Provide a compound wall to cut this extended area from the plot.

6) Additionally, provide a small water tank in the extended South-East area.

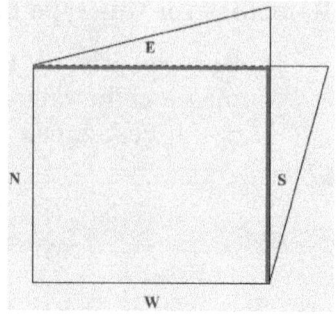

7) Provide a heavy landscape with yellow stones in the extended South-East area.

8) Bury a Cat's eye stone in the extended South-East area to curtail, cut or reduce the additional vibration.

9) Take care of your young growing son. Provide a cosmic *kavach* like rudraksha and auspicious stone with proper mantra to him as guided by an astrologer.

10) Do not use any red colour in this direction; avoid even a tree with red flowers.

4.2 Extensions and cuts in SW zone

Extensions and cuts in SW zone disturb the Earth element, leading to accidents, discontinuity and death of the *grihaswami*.

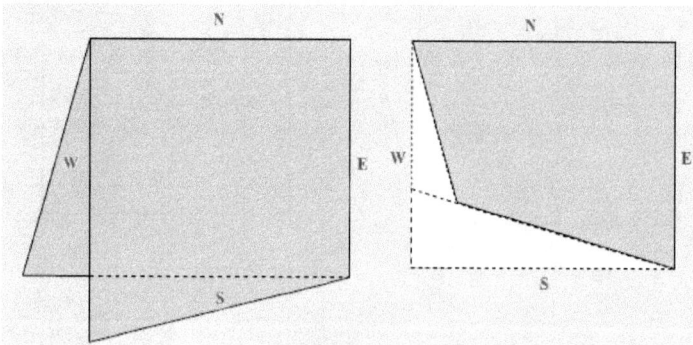

Effects:

* Problems related to court matters, education, business, social prestige, promotion, progress, etc.
* Possibility of accidents and diseases, especially in case of the owner of the house.

Remedies for this problem:

1) Plant an Audumbar tree in this zone and provide a proper platform with yellow stone flooring.

2) Bury a yellow sapphire in this extended zone.

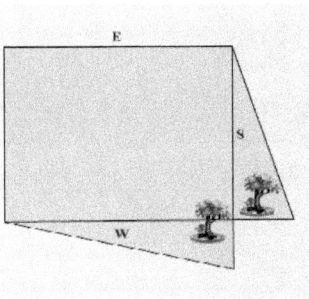

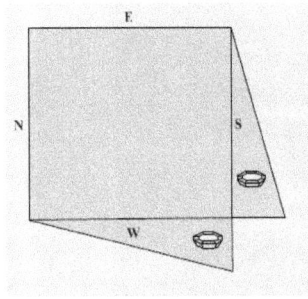

3) Cut this extra space by constructing a right-angled stone compound wall.
4) Provide heavy plantation in the South-West zone.
5) Provide a huge rocky landscape in the extended zone.

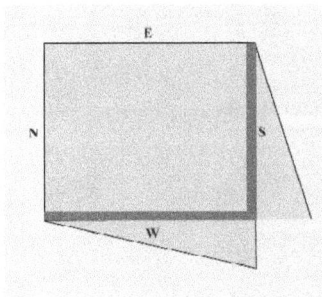

6) Use Jaisalmer Yellow stone in this zone.

7) Construct a pyramidal roof in the extended South-West zone.

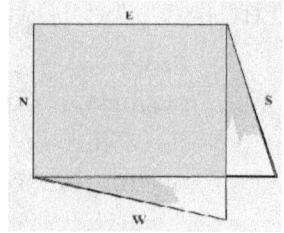

4.3 Extensions and cuts in NW zone

This zone makes the house theft-prone. Labour problems occur very often and trouble from a hidden enemy is also possible.

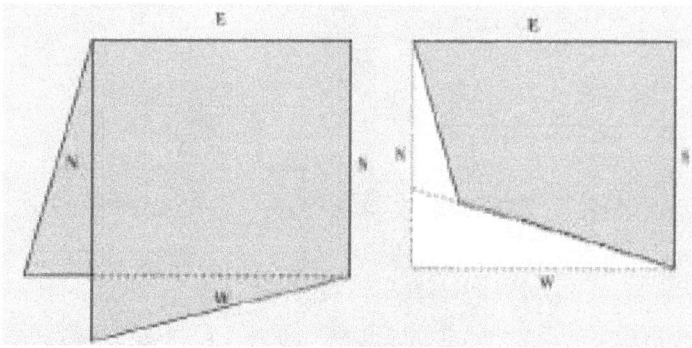

Effects:

* Losses through enemies and servants.
* Obstacles in routine work.
* Displeasure from children.
* Accidents through enemies and servants.

Remedies for this problem :

1) Bury a blue sapphire in the extended North-West zone.

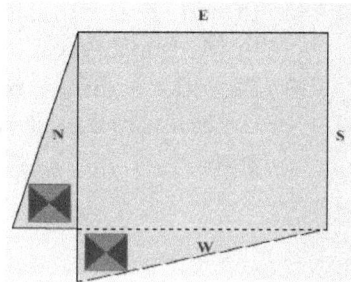

2) Construct a right-angled compound wall to delete the vibration of the extended zone.

3) Provide pyramidal small construction in the extended North-West zone.

4) Provide blue-coloured tiles in the extended North-West zone.

5) Bury brass and lLead in the extended zone.

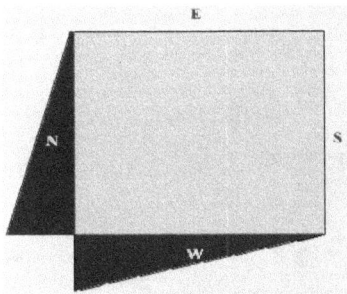

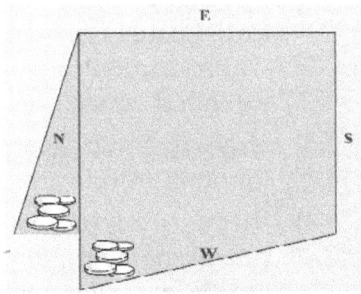

6) A small landscape with blue colour and circular shape, along with bells, gives good results.

7) Encourage regular *pranayam* in young growing daughters of the house.

8) Prolonged resounding *japa* of "SHRIhsssssM" is good for attuning the rhythm of the mind.

4.4 Extensions and cuts in NE zone

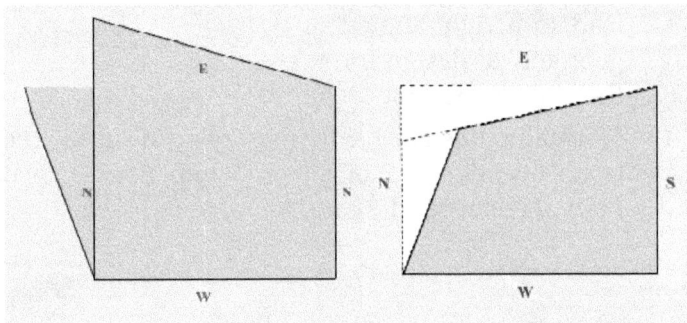

Remedies:

1) Observe this elongated zone carefully to see whether it leads to South-East cut in the plot: if so, then follow the remedies given for the South-East cut.

2) Construct borewells and underground water tanks in this extended zone.

3) Use white marble and fountain in this zone.

4) Bury pearls and rudraksha at 8 points in this extended zone.

5) Bury a silver swastika in this zone.

6) A depression in the ground with a gradual slope towards this extended zone gives good results.

7) Additional depression and water body should lead to a right-angled geometrical design for the rest of the plot.

8) Normally, this extension gives good results if there is an effective use of silver, white marble, water body, crystals and pearls.

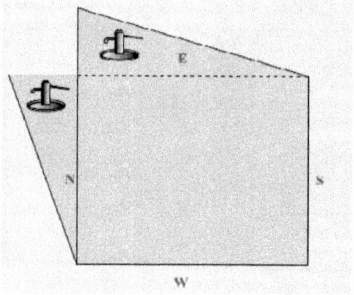

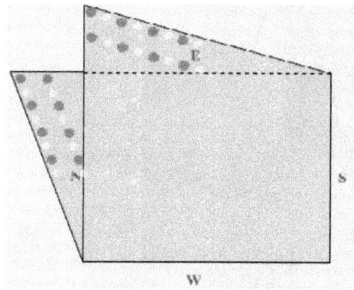

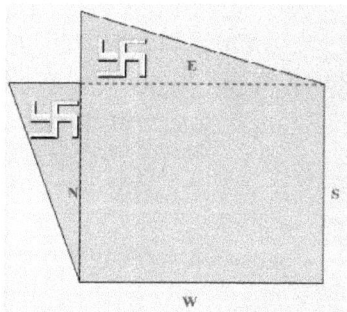

9) If this extension is more than 15 percent area of the plot then treatment of the South-East and North-West zones is necessary to balance the cut pattern.

10) Since this is the main source zone, any extension to it normally gives good results.

House and Zones

5.1 South-West

If the house lies in the SW zone then it acquires all the virtues related to the Earth, leading to stability and prosperity. In the case of such a house, all the 5 great elements play a positive role. All the negative energy counts of S, SW and W get absorbed in the load of the house. Hence, only positive charge acts on the house.

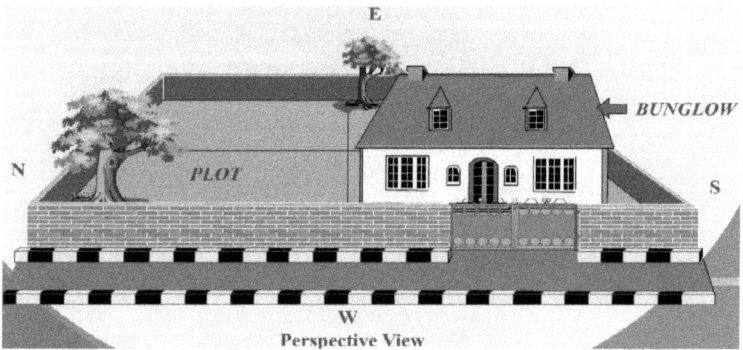

Perspective View

5.2 North-West

If the house lies in the NW zone then it acquires vices related to the Wind element. Very often, such a house gets targeted by dacoits and thieves. On such a house, attacks of S and SE contribute negative energy of count 8. Normally, such houses face problems related to children, and violence related to dacoits and thieves.

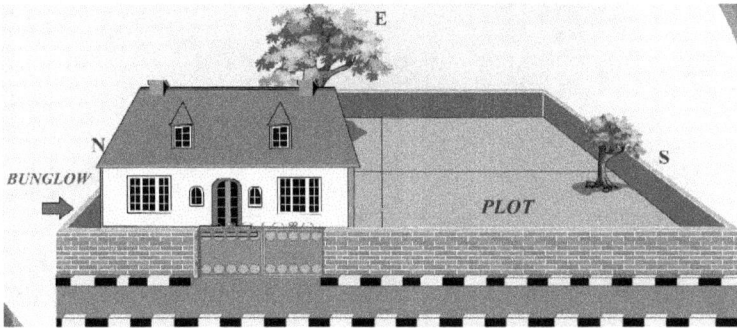

5.3 North-East

If the house lies in the NE zone then such a house represents a haunted house, since all the positive charge of positive deities namely N, NE and E zones gets merged in the load of the house. In such cases, fire in the SE explodes, Yama in the South rules and monster in the SW encroaches the living spaces. The divine deity of NE remains silent and non-cooperative.

5.4 South-East

If the house lies in the SE zone then it represents hazards related to Fire, leading to violence, irritation, worry and insomnia. Such house is under the attack of South-West and West zones contributing 6 and 2 effect. Negative energy always effects by multiplication leading to a total negative attack on such a house of 12 count. This network of negative energy leads to bankruptcy, loss of wealth and violence.

5.5 South and West

Different options while constructing a bungalow in a plot: If the house lies in the S or W zone then the occupant faces mixed results as the negative count gets partially counteracted by the load of the house. On the other hand, occupant enjoys positive results of streaming of organic and *pranik* streams.

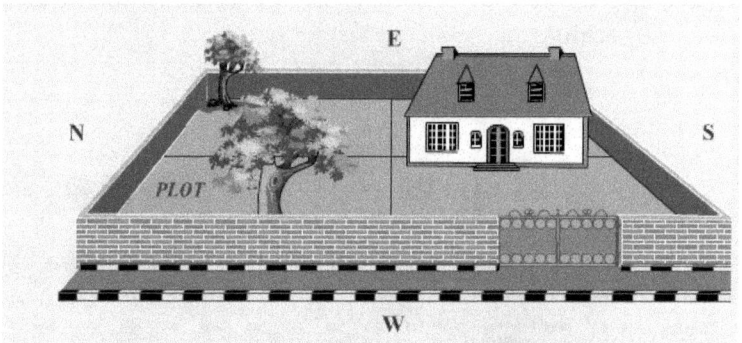

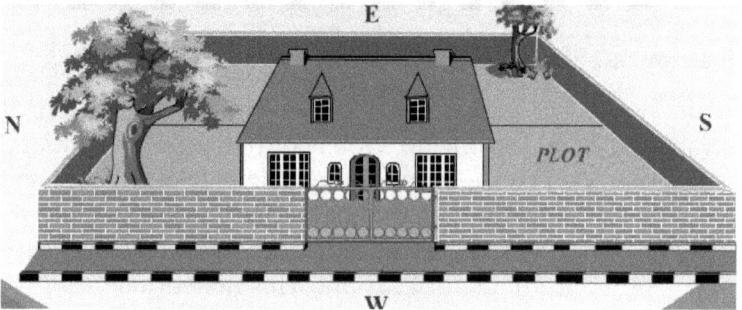

6

Doors and Entrances

Cyclic movement while approaching the house is the key to allocate the position of doors and entrances in traditional science. This is called *'pradakshina marg'*. The second principle is based on least disturbance to the emergence of the power of the 5 great elements. The third principle is based on minimum friction to the stream character of the energy. If this secret of 3 principles is critically observed, then very naturally a *mandalakar* streaming of Chi regulates the bio-magnetic field attached to the house. Violation of any of these 3 principles leads to a failure of energy of the house, where disrupted networks of energy loops loose the power of aspirations.

In such cases, effective measures to correct Vaastu by the use of auspicious stones, colours, herbs, metals, pyramids, specific flooring, fragrances and rituals are necessary.

1) It is customary to divide the side of the plot abutting the road into 9 equal parts. The 4th division from the left while standing inside the plot and facing the road is the most auspicious division to gain the positive charge.

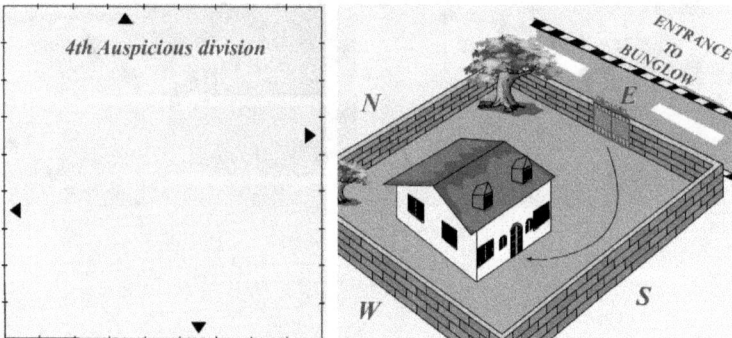

2) It is customary to provide entry to the house in such a way that the way from the plot to the house happens to be clockwise (*pradakshina marg*).

6.1 If plot entry is from South then house entry should be from West.

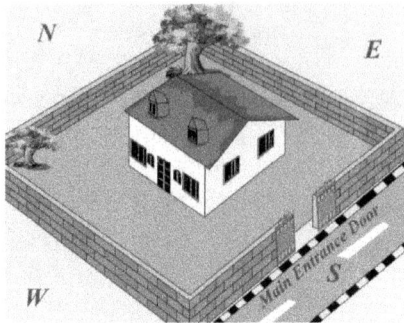

Remedies:

a) Provide blue tile flooring in the entrance lobby which matches the window.

b) Bury 3 green emeralds under this flooring.

c) Bury 2.5kg lead under this flooring.

d) Provide a pyramidal canopy in metal in the entrance zone.

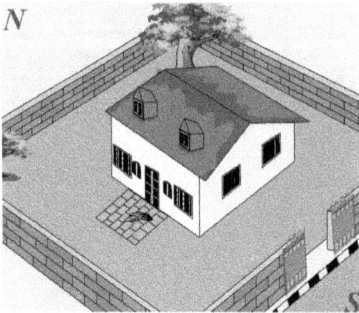

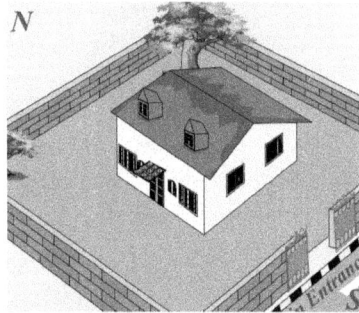

6.2 If plot entry is from West then house entry should be from North.

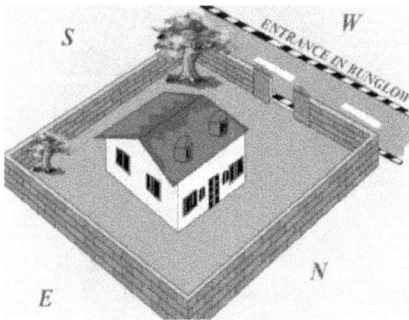

Remedies:

a) Provide white flooring, specifically marble flooring, in the entrance lobby.

b) Bury 81 pearls under this flooring.

c) Bury 50gm silver under this flooring.

d) Do not provide any type of canopy in the North zone as canopy controls and deletes the streaming of energy.

6.3 If plot entry is from East then house entry should be from South.

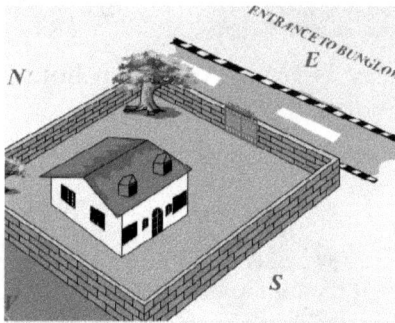

Remedies:

a) Provide Jaisalmer stone in front of the door

b) Bury 5kg lead metal below the Jaisalmer stone.

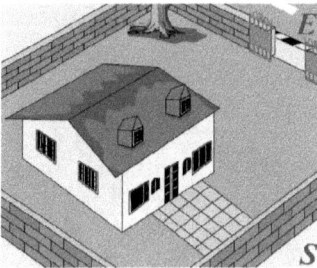

c) Bury 3 blue sapphires below this flooring.

d) Provide pyramidal canopy in deodar wood above the door.

6.4 If plot entry is from North then house entry should be from East

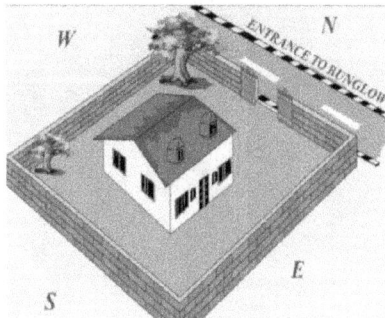

Remedies:

a) Provide wooden or white marble flooring to the entrance zone.

b) Bury 3 crystals under this flooring.

c) Bury 50gm silver under this flooring.

d) Provide copper inlay in a star shape with six apex.

6.5 If house entry is from South-East (plot out of access)

Remedies:

a) Provide pyramidal canopy in wood with 9 pyramids.

b) Provide white marble or wooden flooring in the entrance lobby.

c) Bury 4 red corals in the four corners of the 3 feet by 3 feet entrance zone and bury one yellow sapphire in the center.

d) Bury 4 copper coins each of weight 15gm below each red coral.

6.6 If house entry is from South-West

Remedies:

a) Provide pyramidal canopy in golden or yellow colour.

b) Provide Jaisalmer yellow flooring in the entrance zone.

c) Bury 4 yellow sapphires in the four corners of the 3 feet by 3 feet entrance zone and bury one crystal in the center.

d) Bury 5kg lead metal in the entrance zone.

6.7 If house entry is from North-West

Remedies:

a) Provide pyramidal canopy in white metal.

b) Provide blue tile flooring in the entrance lobby to enhance the power of the Wind element.

28

c) Bury 4 blue sapphires in the four corners of the 3 feet by 3 feet entrance zone and bury one Gomed in the center.

d) Bury 2.5kg lead metal in the entrance zone.

6.8 If house entry is from North-East

a) Provide white marble flooring in the entrance zone.

b) Bury 81 pearls in the center.

c) Bury 50gm silver in the entrance zone.

d) Make a sacred geometry design in the entrance zone using Jaisalmer yellow or green marble.

12 Parameters of Vaastu Rectifications

In modern constructions sometimes it is not possible to have toilets in the Sink zone, windows in Source zone, kitchen in the SE direction or house in the SW zone of the plot. In all such cases it is necessary to use some external media or agency to rectify the energy imbalance of the house. 12 parameters of Vaastu rectifications are nothing but these external media or agencies. These parameters create the *mandalakar* streaming of *pranik* and *jaivik* energy thereby fulfilling the thirst of aspirations leading to flowering and bliss. Such smooth expression of Chi in the environment of the house is the key to attain peace, prosperity and progress. In industries such energies regulate the demand and supply ratio, remove the stagnancies and project the product to the world.

7.1 Colours

White, light blue and light green are the colours of Source quality. Black, yellow, dark blue and brown are the colours of Sink quality. Combination of green and blue, silver and blue, black and white, red and yellow create a progressive streaming of energy where activity, speed and skills attain perfection. Cosmic design based on Yin-Yang theory expresses continuity and completeness. Hence, use white, light blue and light green colours in E, NE and N zones or on E, NE and N walls. Use brown, black, yellow and blue colours with matt finish in S, SW and W zones. Maintain all ceilings in white colour.

7.2. Stone cladding

Since S, SW and W zones are hot and arid, stone cladding on S and SW walls absorb excessive heat and maintain temperature at a moderate level. Since this zone represents the Earth element, such cladding leads to the virtues of the Earth element. When S and SW zones have right expression of the Earth element, the occupant enjoys stability, peace and progress. Where there are faults in the SW zone, stone cladding is the simplest remedy to rectify the Earth reference. One can choose a wide range of colours and types of stones according to the relationship between businesses, planets and the 5 great elements.

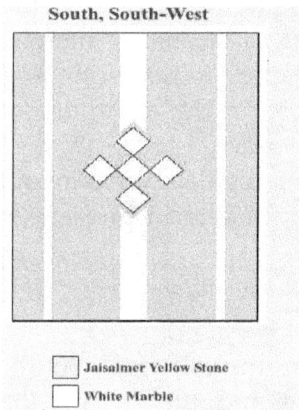

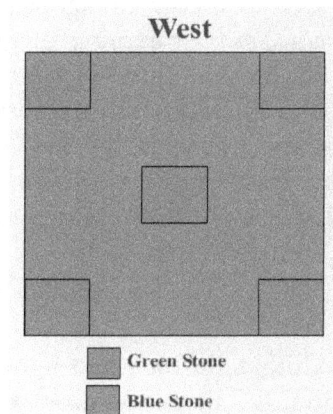

South, South-West

West

Jaisalmer Yellow Stone
White Marble

Green Stone
Blue Stone

Businesses related to Venus can be treated with the use of silver slate stones. Professions related to consultation can be treated with the use of cream and Dholpur stones. As the activity of consultation is related to the planet Jupiter, cream colour helps. Businesses related to advertising and marketing can be treated by the use of flashy colours and contrasts.

7.3 Wooden paneling

Whenever East is closed then to rectify the bio-rhythm of *pranik* energy, wood paneling is the effective remedy. Wood being organic in nature supports the streaming of *pranik* energy. Use of copper foil and crystals will give additional strength to *pranik* energy. As a matter of element of interior decoration, this addition of copper foil, silver foil, crystals and red corals will enhance the aesthetics of the house. Even for the balancing of the SE zone, use of wooden paneling is of great help.

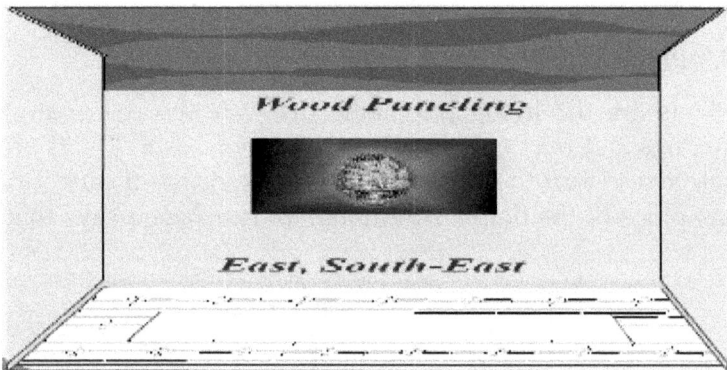

Wood Paneling

East, South-East

7.4 Level difference

For the absorption of the pingala streams Earth is the ideal element. If S, SW and W are devoid of the Earth element, it accelerates the activity of the pingala streams which leads to failure, defeat, disgrace and destruction. In all such cases it is necessary to compensate the load of the Earth element by using the parameter of level difference. Any fault of S, SW and W can be qualitatively cured by raising the S, SW and W zones. Naturally, this creates a slope towards N, NE and E, leading to the acceleration of the moon streams. We know that accelerated N, NE and

E streams shower bliss and order. This parameter reduces the activity of southern streams and enhances the quality of source streams.

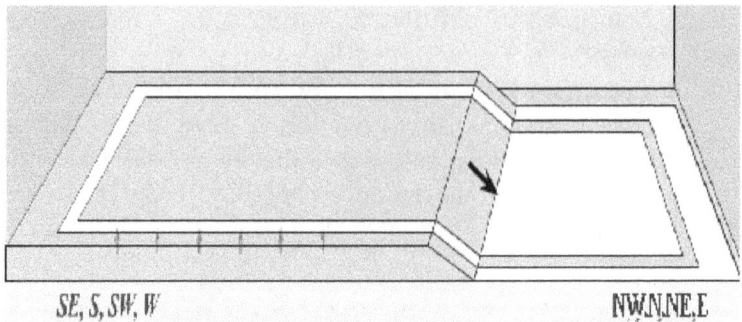

SE, S, SW, W   *NW,N,NE,E*

7.5 Plants

Plants are the living bio-media that can absorb negative streams and may enhance the virtues of Vaastu. Plants are selected to suit the deities of various zones as a carrier of the grace of the deity. Traditional Vaastushastra says that:

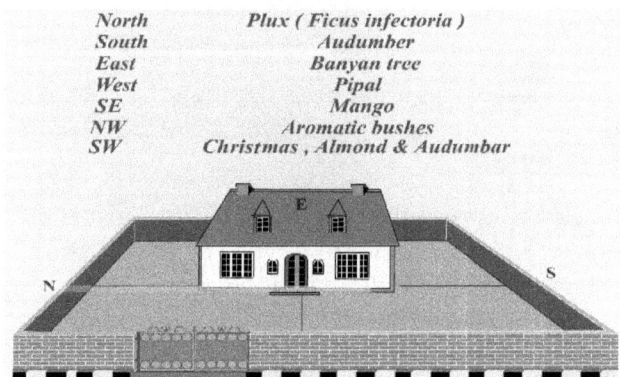

North	Plux (Ficus infectoria)
South	Audumber
East	Banyan tree
West	Pipal
SE	Mango
NW	Aromatic bushes
SW	Christmas , Almond & Audumbar

In general, to reduce the site margin of South and West, a row of ashoka/christmas/almond/eucalyptus trees is of great use to cut the zone of negative energy. Since christmas and almond trees have a pyramidal shape, they have a powerful potential to absorb the pingala streams. Radioactive rays of the scorching sun can be kept away

34

using the row of these pyramidal trees. Occimum Sanctum, i.e. Tulsi is considered a source of divine *pranik* energy. One can use the Tulsi plant in all directions and may circle the house in the orbit of *prana*. Similarly, coconut trees being *Kalpavriksh* are allowed in all directions. In astrology, each constellation is assigned a particular plant, which acts as a carrier of its grace. It is called the *Aaradhyavriksh*. According to the constellation of *grihaswami*, worship of the *Aaradhyavriksh* gives multiple cosmic benefits. If any plant casts shadow on the house then it reduces the streaming of positive energy. Hence, it is advisable to chop the branches of such trees, particularly if they lie in NE, N, NW and E zones, i.e. source zones. As a matter of cosmic grace, use of bonsai plants also gives the same effect.

7.6 False ceiling

Forms like pyramids have a cosmic power which can control the aspiration, confine the zone and curtail the excessive expansion of negative energy. In terms of form, pyramid is of sink nature. Pyramid holds the zone, limits the spread of negative energy, and acts as a powerful media to cut the extensions to regulate the squarish shape of the house – pyramid acts like a key. To rectify the entrances, pyramids can be used to control the negative stream. In all such cosmic corrections of entrances pyramids play a great positive role. Due to the sink nature of pyramid, its use is restricted to the sink zones only, i.e. false ceiling in pyramids is applicable to SE, S, SW and W zones. One should select the colour and shape of the pyramid according to the element of the direction. As the subject has already been discussed in detail in the chapters related to entrances and terraces, a short reference is enough. Use of cut pyramids, domes and cylindrical shells are popular remedies to enhance the energy content.

Uses of false ceiling:

a) Entrances in the sink zone.

b) To cut the extension/balconies in the sink zones.

For example:

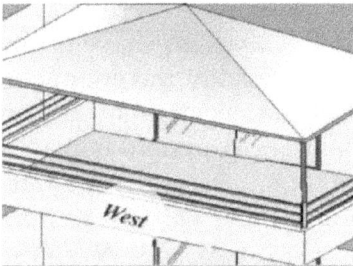

    1. Terraces in SE

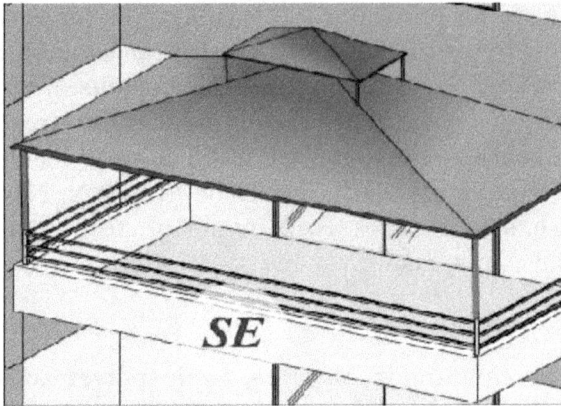

2. Terraces in West   3. Terraces in SW

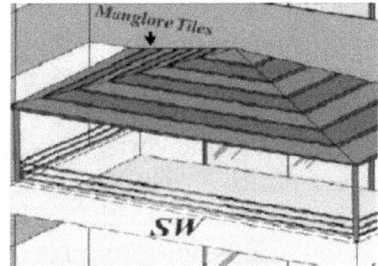

7.7 Metals

Each metal has some connectivity to planets and particular elements. This particular virtue is of great importance to enhance the aspiration, regulate the *mandalakar* streaming of energy, and absorb the force of negative energy. Certain metals have specific qualities of absorption, i.e. they are of

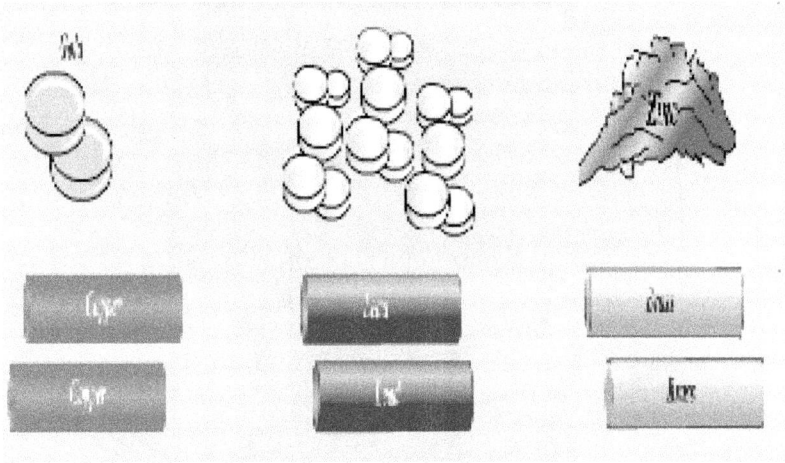

sink nature, whereas certain metals have a divine virtue of glorifying the aspiration of positive zones.

Lead is equated with Saturn and Rahu.

Silver is equated with Moon, Venus and Mercury.

Copper is equated with Mars and Sun.

Zinc is equated with Jupiter.

Brass is equated with Mercury.

Gold is equated with Sun and Jupiter.

As regards elemental classification, Lead is equated with the Earth element, Copper with the Fire element, Silver with the Water element, and White metal with the Wind element. Enhancement of Source-direction, confinement and curtailment of Sink-direction is the basic purpose of Vaastushastra. This principle is followed while applying the treatment of metals in zones and directions. In Jainism and Hinduism, *kilak* (nails) is used to remove evil powers and ghosts.

1. Extensions and cuts in the SW

    * Bury 9 nails of lead weighing 2.5kg each in a ascending geometry.

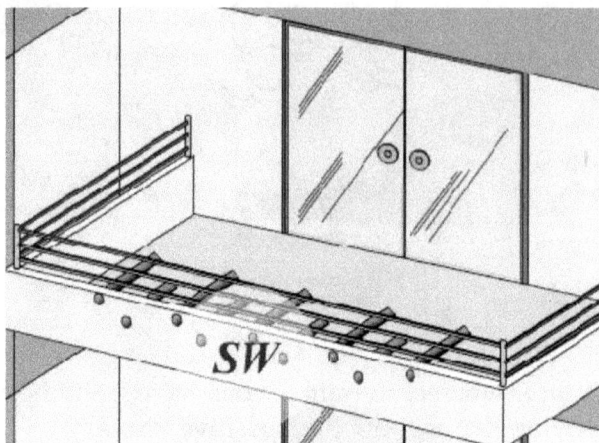

2. Extensions and cuts in the West

    * Bury 7 nails of lead weighing 1.5kg each in a ascending geometry.

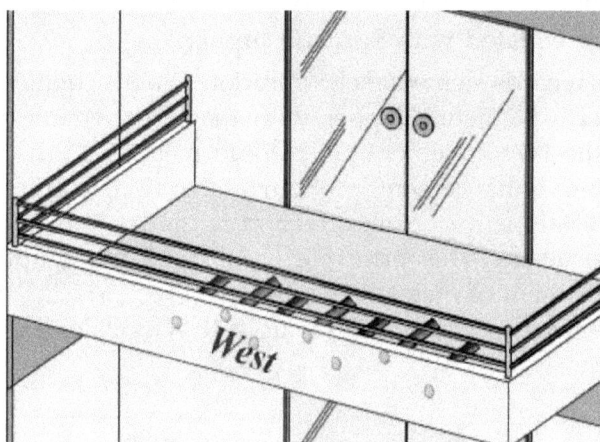

7.8 Shanku Sthapana (Forms and Pyramids)

In modern constructions hardly any house is built according to the tenets of Vaastushastra. But it is not always possible to change the zones of the toilets, or the position of the kitchen, or the position of the entrances. Though the theory represents correct sacred cuts for entrances, in modern architecture it is not possible to use such divisions. In such situations *Shanku Sthapana* or use of forms and pyramids is a simple remedy to balance the 5 great elements. Square pyramid represents the Earth element, triangular pyramid represents the Fire element, and conical/circular pyramid represents the Wind element. Since pyramid acts as a controller of elements, it is a simple medium to balance the aura of the 5 great elements.

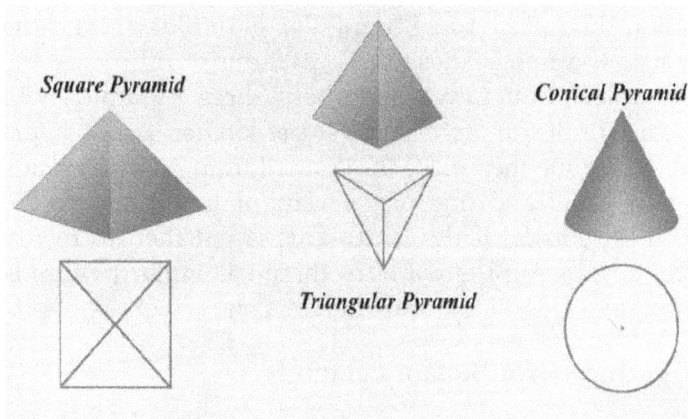

Square Pyramid

Conical Pyramid

Triangular Pyramid

Circular pyramids are used for North-West corner.

These pyramids rectify irregularities and create balance of the five great elements.

If a ritual is performed in an auspicious time, i.e. *muhurth,* then divine virtue descends in these pyramids and acts like the great *digbandhan.*

7.8.1 Examples for Triangular Pyramids

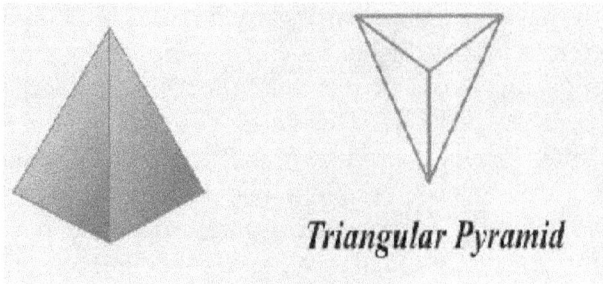

Triangular Pyramid

Whenever SE, SW and NW zones, i.e. Nanda, Bhadra and Jaya, are irregular due to geometry or due to the loss of element then these pyramids act as a tool for correction. In general, two triangular pyramids are used to rectify the SE corner.

If either the door or the toilet is in the South-East direction then place three triangular pyramids around the door and the toilet. These three pyramids will rectify the reference of Agni tatwa and these three pyramids will create a wonderful *digbandhan*. If the kitchen is not in the South-East zone then place three small triangular pyramids along the wall and one mega triangular pyramid in the South-East corner. If the South-East is cut then to rectify the balance of Agni tatwa bury three triangular pyramids in triangular geometry near the cut zone.

7.8.2 Examples for Square Pyramids

Two square pyramids are used to rectify the SW zone.

These pyramids rectify the imbalance of the Earth Element.

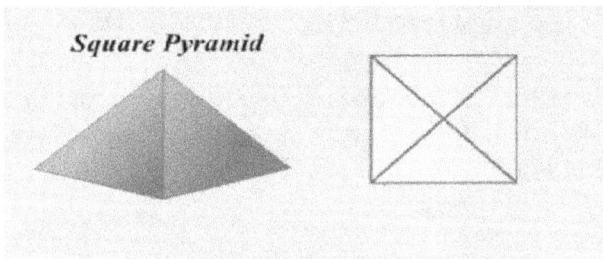

Square Pyramid

7.8.3 Examples for Circular Pyramids

Two circular pyramids are used for the NW corner.

These pyramids rectify irregularities and create balance of the five great elements. If a ritual is performed in an auspicious time, i.e. *muhurth,* then divine virtue descends in these pyramids and acts like the great *digbandhan.*

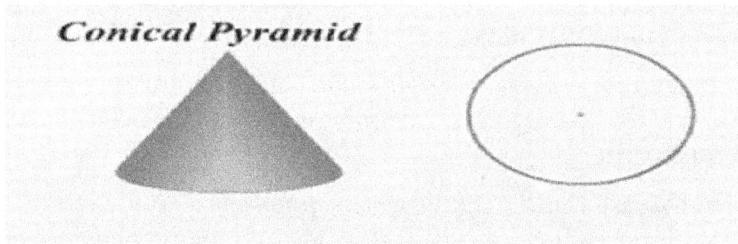

Conical Pyramid

7.9 Yoga

The effect of Vaastu does not flower into a success unless the inner spaces of a human being are cleared and purified. Faults of each direction create a negative mark called cosmic poison in a person. To eradicate this cosmic poison, a different tool of yoga, and worship of different deities are needed.

Vibrations, waves, sound and light are powerful tools to eradicate this cosmic poison.

S and SW faults: Do *Sudarshan Kriya* founded by Sri Sri Ravishankar, as this is a rhythmic dynamic breathing technique and showers rhythmic bliss and synchronicity on the being. Poison of SW is a deep-rooted seed; so to eradicate this poison, regularity is must in *Sudarshan Kriya.*

West faults: Do Reiki and *pranik*-healing as this fault leads to a disorder and irregularity in behavior. A comparative passive technique is needed.

North-West fault: Technique of breathing regulates the mind, disciplines the nature and creates positive thought in intelligence. As faults in the NW are related to moon and mind, psychological disorders are a common complaint related to NW faults.

North faults: This fault is related to the mind and ladies of the house. To create harmony and to regulate energy streaming follow *Vipassana* techniques. This is a passive technique and will regulate the organic body of the being.

East faults: Do *bhasrika pranayam*. This dynamic breathing technique will regulate the streams of *prana* in body, mind and intellect.

South-East faults: Do *kapalbhati pranayam*. This rhythmic breathing technique will create positive loops of *prana* in the voids of being. It has direct effect on the '*Nabhi-Chakra*'. So Agni tatwa (Surya) – fire – in the body is balanced by this technique.

7.10 Windows and Doors

Windows and doors are like the eyes and ears of the house. As a general formula, the ratio for N, E, W, S should be 4:3:2:1, i.e. North should have 4 windows, East should have 3 windows, West should have 2 windows and South should have 1 window. This is the ideal proportion. This formula forces the energy to travel in a *mandalakar* way. Windows in the South and windows in the West allow light in the house from the sink zones. So they spread negative energy in the house. Windows in the South should have yellow glass. This colour represents the Earth element. Earth element in South accelerates the organic streams of North. Windows in the West should have blue glass. Wind element in the West energises the house by activity and strength. Blue represents the Wind element. Use pyramidal chhajjas in the South and the West windows as pyramid controls negative energy, curtails Vikshep deity and holds the Saturn effect.

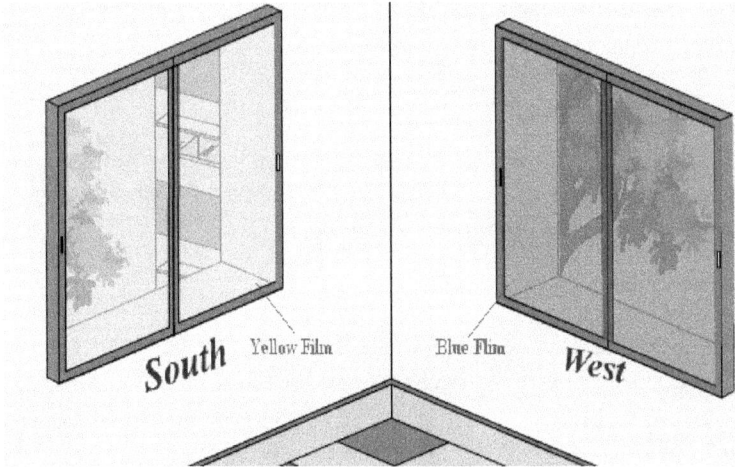

South   Yellow Film   Blue Film   West

7.11 Use of Precious Stones (Ratnadhyay)

Precious stones virtually transform the earthly house into a divine, celestial form. Eight directions are focused to give vibrations of 8 aspirations. Home becomes a miniature solar system due to which it attains the power of planets in the appropriate zones and directions. It creates a *mandal*, a helical path, through which energy gets regulated to attain divinity. Some precious stones are of Yin virtue and some have a Yang virtue. Stones with Yang quality are used in the Source zone and stones with Yin quality are used in the Sink zones.

Ruby

Ruby is placed in the central zone to stimulate the power of 8 directions. Ruby adds the power of Aakash tatwa, i.e. Space to the Earth element, eye of Yang in the body of Yin, i.e. earth, creates a Tai-Chi. Divine verse says *"Madhya me Padmaragan tu."*

Red Coral

Red coral in the East zone adds shine and strength to the flame of Mars which, in turn, blesses health, power, strength and courage.

Yellow Sapphire

Yellow sapphire in the South-East zone controls the intense explosive form of fire in the South-East zone. This controls anger, ego and stroke of violence.

Cat's Eye

Cat's eye in the South zone controls the sun stream, curtails Yama and cuts the anti-clockwise loops of negative energy.

Crystal

Crystal in the South-West zone adds a divine virtue to the Earth element. Since this is the place of romance, virtue of Venus regulates the rhythm.

Blue Sapphire

Blue sapphire in the West zone counteracts the negative energy of the sinking zone. It represents Vaayu tatwa (wind) due to its colour. So it controls the Wind element and protects the house from disagreement. Blue sapphire in the NW zone controls the excessive streaming of the Moon element. A disciplined mind and ordered Moon element are positive reflections of the NW zone which are attended to by placing a blue sapphire in the NW zone.

Green Emerald

Green emerald in the North zone creates oneness of mind and intelligence. It is the place of Kuber, the deity of wealth. Green emerald represents Mercury, a friend of Kuber.

Pearls

Pearls in the NE zone enhance the virtue of the Water element, thereby regulating cosmic energy in the NE zone. Pearls represent moon and moon represents the divine reflection of the Water element.

7.12 Yantra

Yantra is a sacred geometry of the 5 great elements and their forms. *Shivlinga* is also a form of *yantra* with a mystical matrix that maintains order.

7.12.1 Ishanya Patra

Ishanya Patra lights the entire zone of energy. It is the assembly of silver, crystal, mirror, *Shri Yantra, Shiv Yantra,* water and flow of water. NE represents the confluence of divine powers which transforms the Jal tatwa into *Teerth* (Divine Water). Crystal polarises divine energy and focuses intelligence and mind. Silver promotes virtue of moon. Mirror enhances the aspirations of the direction.

Ishanya Patra

7.12.2 Shashi Bhooshan

It is a stone pedestal with square pyramid on the top. Square pyramid has *mantra beej 'Gam'* which stabilises the quality of Earth in the SW zone. A powerful Earth element in the SW zone

Shashi Bhooshan

absorbs all the negative energies and in turn regulates the *mandalakar* form of energy that flowers the aspirations of all directions. Helical flow of organic and *pranik* streams create sacred patterns and forms where all the deities stay, flower and bless. One Shashi Bhooshan in the SW corner takes care of the entire space and all the zones.

7.12.3 Disc of Saturn

It is the yantra of the West surface. One disc of Saturn with blue crystal enhances the Aaditya stream of the East zone. West is a sink direction and Saturn in the West horizon gives power to aspirations of the East and West zones. It is made up of lead and blue crystals. Lead absorbs all the subatomic particles and purifies the zone. Blue crystals enhance the virtue of Vaayu tatwa, i.e. the Wind element. One disc of Saturn on the West surface removes all disagreements from life, creates order in behaviour, rhythm in life and virtue in status.

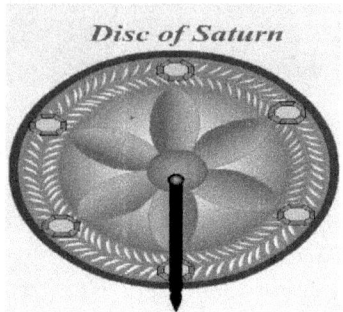

7.12.4 Bhoum Yantra (Mystic of Mars)

It represents the order and virtue of Mars. Mars has qualities of Earth and the power of Fire, i.e. Agni. Mars is the chief commander and warrior of divine deities. It is comprised of copper which has divine virtue of sanctity. Copper is a good conductor of energy and absorbs all the eddy currents of South leading

46

to a regular *mandalakar* streaming of cosmic energy. A *Bhoum Yantra* on the South wall eradicates the possibility of all negative energies.

21 Severe Faults (*Mahadosh*) and Remedies

Wells, borewells and depressions add virtue and quality to source zones, but in sink zones they activate negative energy and create loops and networks of sinking forces in an anti-clockwise rhythm. Hence, wells, borewells and depressions are good in NW, N and NE zone. But in E, SE, S, SW and W they disturb the energies of Vaastu.

8.1 Well or borewell in the SE corner

This disturbs the hormonal cycle of the males of the house leading to impotency, loss of children, accidents and fire hazards. It is advised to refill the well by concrete/stones/sand/murram, preferably do a ritual called Kup-shanti, before refilling the well. Bury 7 red corals and 3 yellow sapphires in this zone. A long stay in such faulty house may

make severe damage at the aura level. A compensation for this diseased aura could be done by the regular exercise of 'bhasrika' (a breathing technique). Additionally, it is advised to drink gold water early in the morning. In consultation with an Ayurveda expert, use of herbs like *ashwagandha*, etc. will be of great help in rectifying the aura.

In case the refilling of well is not possible then following alternatives can be used:

a) Bury 3 triangular copper pyramids of 12″ side between the house and the well with proper ritual.

b) Plant a mango tree between the well and the house.

c) Place pet animals, e.g. cow, dog and buffalos between the house and the well.

d) Provide a pyramidal cover in copper metal above the borewell.

e) If possible, cut the well from the house by constructing a compound wall.

8.2 Well or borewell in the South and SW zones

This creates depression in the main sink zone due to which devastating negative energy encroaches the house, leading to death, destruction, demolition and discontinuity. Instances of accidents and murder are higher if the well is situated in South. Similarly, instances of accidents and suicides are higher if the well is in the South-West zone. It is advisable to avoid any remedies related to this fault and refill the borewell as early as possible, preferably by concrete/stones/sand/murram. One should also perform a ritual called *Kup-shanti*, before refilling the well. Bury 7 blue sapphires if the well is in the South zone. If the well is in the SW zone, bury 25 kg lead in this zone. A long stay in such faulty house may cause severe damage to the people living in the house. This fault specifically hits the *grihaswami*/father, i.e. males in the age-bracket of 30 to 50 years. If this cosmic poison is absorbed over a long period of time then it is advised to learn and follow the dynamic breathing technique *Sudarshan kriya* founded by Sri Sri Ravishankar. This being a rhythmic dynamic breathing technique removes the cosmic poisons from body, mind and intellect very effectively.

In case refilling the well is not possible then:

a) Bury 4 square copper pyramids of 12″ side with proper ritual between the house and the well.

b) Plant one Audumber tree between the well and the house.

c) Place pet animals, e.g. cow, dog and buffaloes between the house and the well.

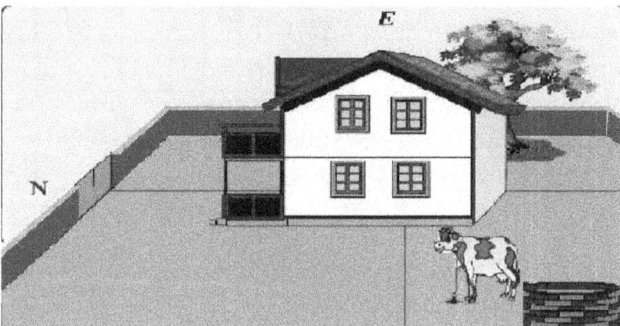

d) Provide a pyramidal cover in copper metal above the borewell.

e) If possible cut the well from the house by constructing a compound wall.

f) Bury 9 nails of steel (2.5kg each) in ascending geometry between the well and the house.

8.3 Well or borewell in the West zone

This is the zone of Saturn and Mercury. Hence, any disturbance in this zone leads to defeat, disagreement in life and derailment of brain activity. This zone is traditionally termed as *Rangashala* and the deity of this zone is 'Varun'. Borewell or well in this zone disturbs married life, partnerships and court matters. It is advised to avoid any remedies related to this fault and refill the borewell as early as possible with concrete/stones/sand/murram.

It is also advised to perform a ritual called Kup-shanti. Bury 7 green emeralds and 3 blue sapphires. Bury 7 steel rods (5' long 2" diameter) in this zone. A long stay in such faulty house may cause severe damage to the personality and character of the *grihaswami*. To eradicate the effect of long stay in such a house it is helpful to do a course named *'Siddh Samadhi Yoga'* founded by Sri Rishi Prabhakar. Incase refilling the well is not possible then following alternatives need to be followed:

a) Bury 2 circular copper pyramids of 12" diameter with proper ritual between the house and the well.

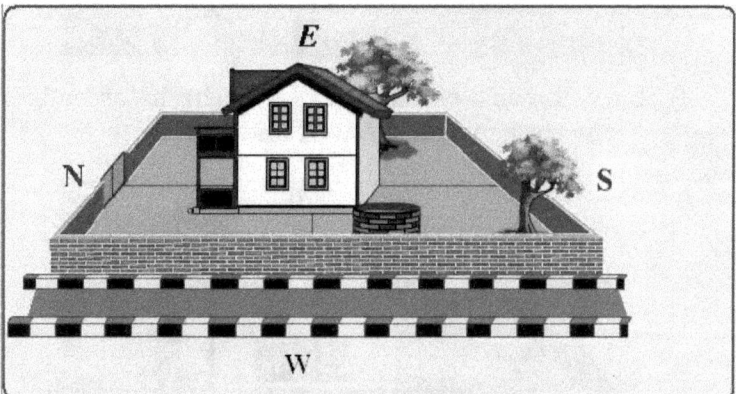

b) Plant one peepal tree between the well and the house.

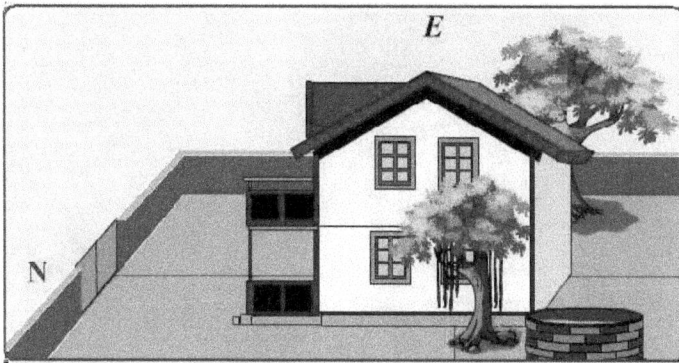

c) Place pet animals, e.g. cow, dog and buffaloes between the house and the well.

d) Provide a conical pyramidal cover in white metal above the borewell.

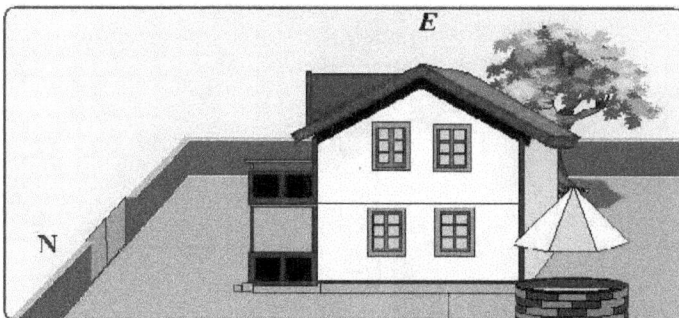

e) If possible cut the well from the house by constructing the compound wall.

f) Bury 7 nails of steel (5" long and 2' diameter) in ascending geometry between the well and the house.

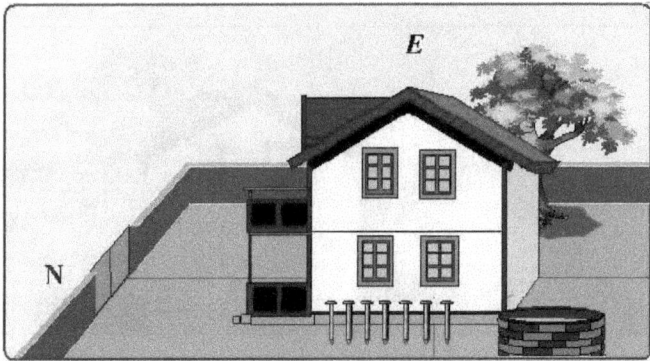

8.4. Well or borewell in the East zone

Depression in this zone is a positive thing but water in this zone disturbs the quality of the Fire element. This is the zone of Mars, Venus and Sun. Hence, any disturbance in this zone leads to cowardice, idleness and fear. This zone is traditionally termed *Adityashala* and the deity of this zone is *Aaditya*. Borewell or well in this zone disturbs the Fire element and flame of this zone.

It is advisable to refill the well with concrete/stones/ sand/murram. Preferably, do a ritual called *Kup-shanti*, before refilling the well. Bury 7 crystals and 3 red corals. Bury 50gm of silver and 200gm of copper rods in a star shape with 6 apex points. A long stay in such faulty house may lead to *putranash,* i.e. loss of son. To eradicate the effects of long stay in such a house it is helpful to chant '*Surya Kavach*', *Aditya Hriday* or do *kapalbhati*. In case refilling the well is not possible then:

a) Bury 20gm copper coins at six apex points in a star shape in the East zone.

b) Plant one Vat tree between the well and the house.

c) Place a cow between the house and the well.

d) Provide a cylindrical cover in copper metal above the borewell.

Road hitting on Vaastu

In traditional language this fault is called *Vidhi-shula*. *Vidhi* means road and *shula* means hitting. In Feng-Shui it is a belief that deities and angels travel in a *mandalakar* path, i.e. logarithmic helical path, and bad spirits and ghosts travel in an intense straight channel. In a way *vidhi-shula* is the extension of this belief.

A straight, intense and forceful travel of energy is like high-voltage shock to a Vaastu. Such force acts like a killing force and disturbs the deities and aspirations of all directions. Some modern Vaastu experts believe that *vidhi-shula* from source zones, i.e. N, NE and E creates a positive result, but arrow hitting from frontside or backside is bound to create wounds in the body. Traditional Vaastu does not support this belief of modern Vaastu experts.

8.5 Road hitting from the East (*Purva Vidhi-shula*)

East represents Mars and Venus so the effect of *purva vidhi-shula* leads to arrogance, immorality, hardness in nature and inhuman character. People living in such houses tend to be violent in nature.

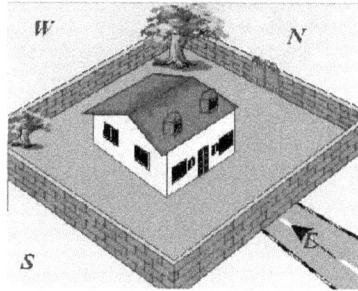

This *vidhi-shula* may lead to the loss of sons. In East, fire represents flame, but *vidhi-shula* turns the flame into an explosion.

Remedies

a) Plant a big banyan tree in the confluence zone of the road and Vaastu.

b) Provide a bulging compound in wood and white stones to negate the hitting force of this *vidhi-shula*.

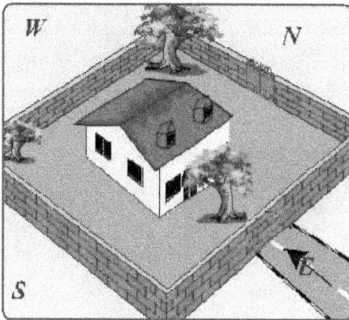

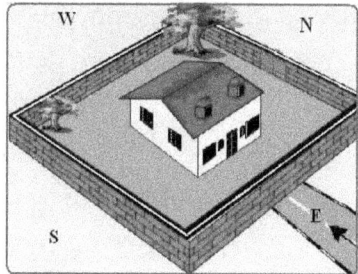

c) Use circular pieces of mirror on compound wall to distract the hitting force.

d) Provide a fireplace in the confluence zone of the road and Vaastu.

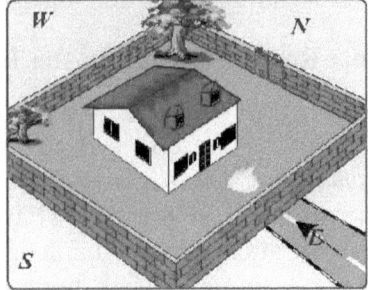

e) Provide a bulging circular surface in copper with spearheads on the surface.

f) Provide a big sinking depression, i.e. pit in the confluence zone of the road and Vaastu.

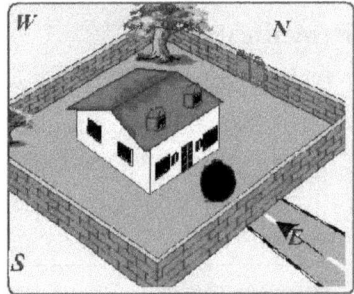

8.6 Road hitting from the South-East *(Aagneya Vidhi-shula)*

South-East represents patterns of intense fire waiting for explosion and violence. If possible, leave such a house or do not select such a plot.

Traditional theory says that this fault results in destruction of the

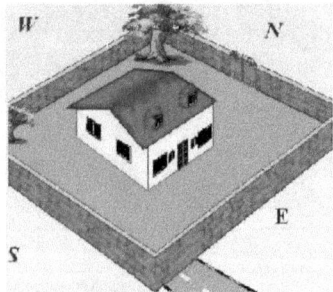

60

whole family, i.e. *kula-kshay*. All kinds of losses, bankruptcy, family disturbance, etc. results due to this fault.

Remedies

a) Plant a big mango tree in the confluence zone of the road and Vaastu.

b) Provide a bulging compound in brown stone to negate the hitting force of *vidhi-shula*.

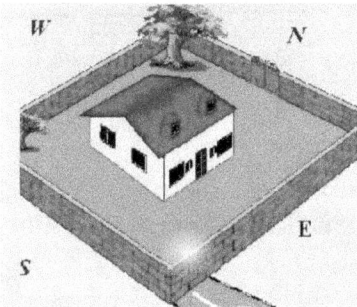

c) Use circular intense white lights to distract the hitting force.

d) Provide a small pond with fountain and lights in the confluence zone of the road and Vaastu.

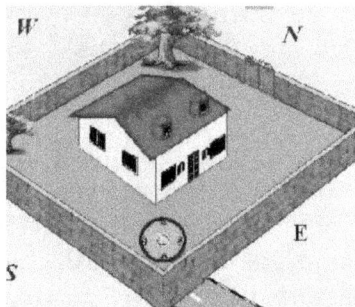

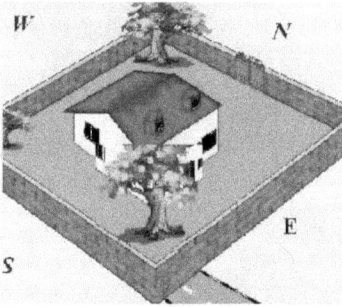

e) Provide a bulging circular surface in white metal with spearheads on the surface.

f) Provide a small mount in landscaping with a christmas tree at the center of the confluence zone of the road and Vaastu.

8.7 Road hitting from the South *(Dakshin Vidhi-shula)*

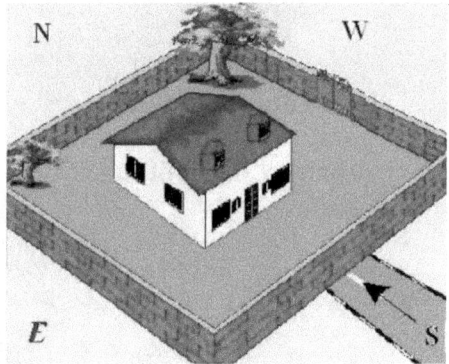

This is the worst amongst all the faults and wipes out the entire living experience of the family. The devastating dance of Shiva eradicates life at all levels since Yama is the deity of this direction. Do not dare to live in such a house. Traditional theory terms this fault as *Yama-Vidhi*. Only criminals, prostitutes and gamblers can withstand the poison of this evil force. This fault results in the destruction of the whole family, i.e. *kula-kshay*. All kinds of losses, bankruptcy, family disturbances, etc. result due to this fault.

a) Plant a big Audumber tree in the confluence zone of the road and Vaastu.

b) Provide a bulging compound in heavy stone with raised heights to negate the hitting force of *vidhishula*.

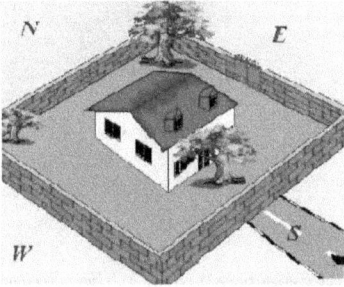

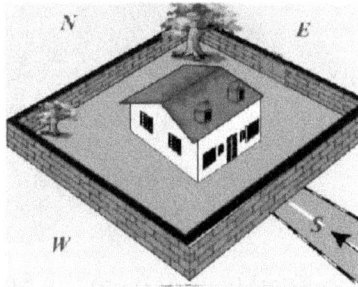

c) Use circular intense yellow lights to distract the hitting force.

d) Provide a small mount in landscaping with an almond tree in the confluence zone of the road and Vaastu.

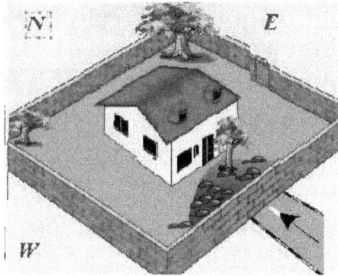

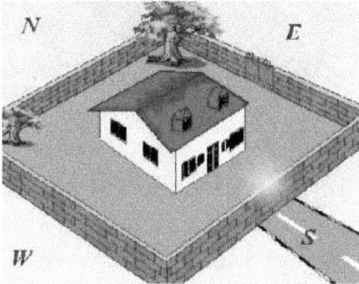

e) Provide a bulging circular surface in lead metal with spearheads on the surface.

f) Plant 9 christmas trees in a convex curvature with bulge projecting towards the hitting force.

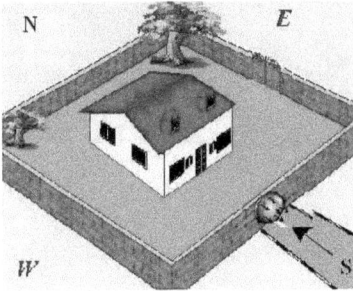
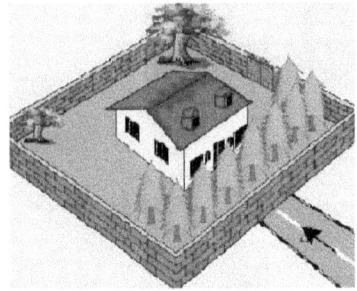

8.8 Road hitting from the South-West (*Nairutya Vidhi-shula*)

This is the worst amongst all the faults and wipes out the entire living experience of the family. The devastating dance of Shiva eradicates life at all levels since Yama is the deity of this direction. Do not dare to live in such a house. Traditional theory terms this fault as *Mrutu-Vidhi*. Only criminals, prostitutes and gamblers can withstand the poison of this evil force. This fault results in the destruction of the whole family. All types of losses, bankruptcy, family disturbances, etc. result due to this fault.

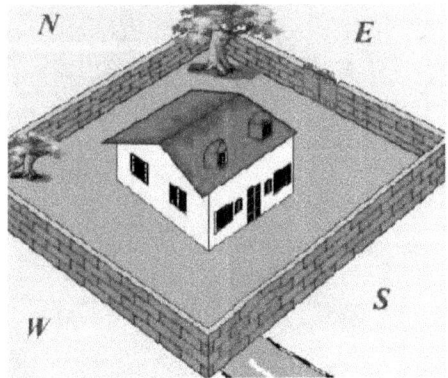

Remedies

a) Plant a big Audumber tree in the confluence zone of the road and Vaastu.

b) Provide a bulging compound in heavy stone with raised heights to negate the hitting force of Vidhi-shula.

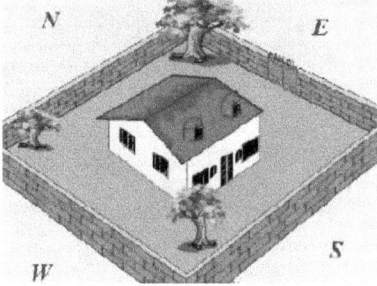

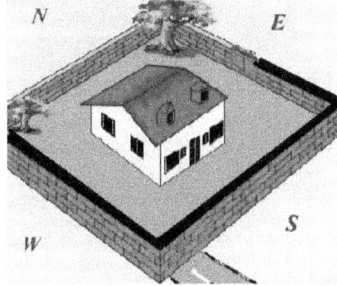

c) Construct a towering L- shaped stone wall to cut the reference of the SW zone.

d) Use circular intense yellow lights to distract the hitting force.

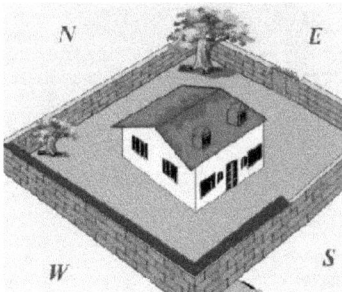

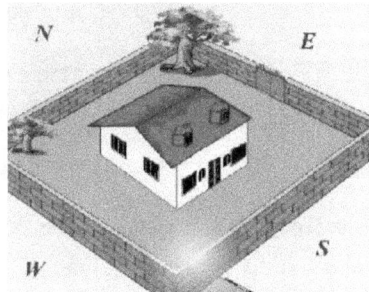

e) Provide a small mount in landscaping with an almond tree in the confluence zone of the road and Vaastu.

f) Provide a bulging circular surface in lead metal with spearheads on the surface.

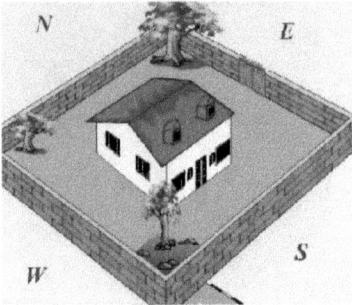

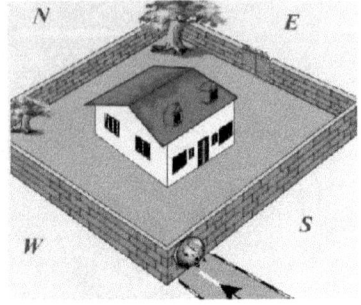

g) Plant 9 christmas trees in a convex curvature with bulge projecting towards the hitting force.

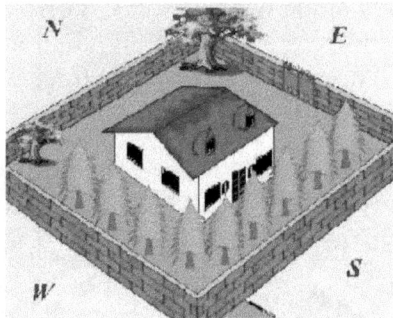

8.9 Road hitting from the West *(Paschim Vidhi-shula)*

This is the zone of Saturn and Mercury, hence any disturbance in this zone leads to defeat, disagreement in life and derailment of brain activity. This zone is traditionally termed as *Rangashala* and the deity of this zone is 'Varun'. It particularly disturbs married life, partnerships and court

matters. Traditional theory terms this fault as *Varun-Vidhi*. This fault results in the destruction of the whole family, i.e. *kula-kshay*. Business losses, disturbance in married life, defeat in court matters, disagreement in every walk of life and end of family are the effects of this *vidhi-shula*.

Remedies

a) Plant a big Pipal tree in the confluence zone of the road and Vaastu.

b) Provide a bulging compound for joints in heavy stone with lead metal to negate the hitting force of *vidhi-shula*.

c) Use circular intense blue lights to distract the hitting force.

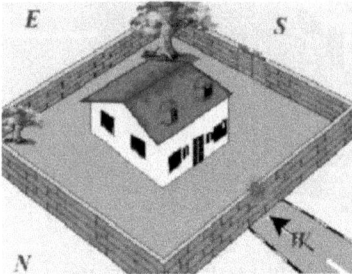

d) Provide a small mount in landscaping with a christmas tree in the confluence zone of the road and Vaastu.

e) Provide a bulging circular surface in lead metal with spearheads on the surface.

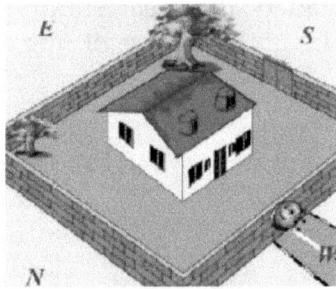

8.10 Road hitting from the North-West (*Vayavya Vidhi-shula*)

North-West represents moon and the active Wind element. Effects of this *vidhi-shula* range from disturbance in mind, bad influence on the character of daughters, general progeny, addictions and attachment to external forces. Evil forces in the outer orbit of the NW zone are termed as *Paaprakshasi*. Due to *vidhi-shula*, this evil agent becomes hyperactive and disturbs the sanctity of the house.

Remedies

a) Erect a metal tower and hang bells to distract the hitting vibration.

b) Provide a small pond with blue lotus flowers in it. Provide blue lights in the confluence zone of the road and Vaastu.

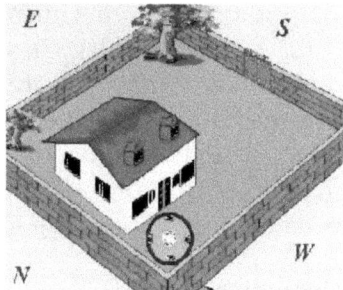

c) Provide a fireplace in the confluence zone of the road and Vaastu.

d) Provide a bulging circular surface in lead with spearheads on the surface.

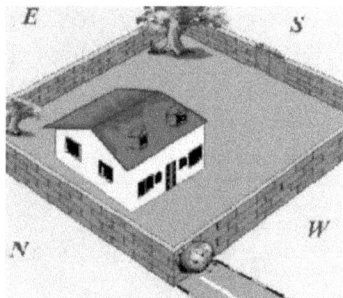

e) Provide a big sinking depression, i.e. pit in the confluence zone of the road and Vaastu.

8.11 Road hitting from the North *(Uttar Vidhi-shula)*

Comparatively, this fault leads to the least disturbance. The end of family line may happen due to the birth of daughters only, but never by violence. Sometimes due to over-religious nature, one may ignore practical thought. Due to such *vidhi-shula*, people may also become shy, inactive and god-fearing. Such people may encounter problems due to their simple and straight behaviour. Traditionally, this vidhi-shula is called *Som-Vidhi*.

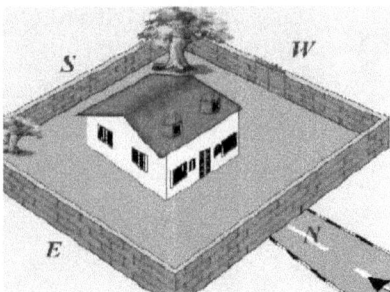

Remedies

a) Provide a lunar-shaped water body, finished in white marble, with bulge projecting towards the hitting side of the road.

b) Provide 9 borewells in lunar shape in the North zone with bulge projecting towards hitting side of the road.

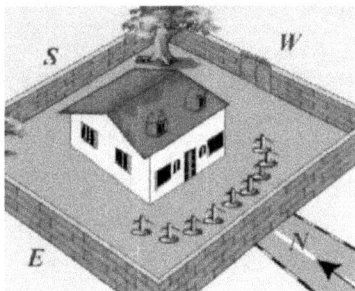

Common faults in modern flats

New architecture is based on asymmetry and non-grid planning. This style of architecture does not follow any discipline, order or environmental constraints. These

70

buildings are nothing but a nuisance to human habitat. In tropical countries, high thermal torque and solar radiation lead to various kinds of diseases due to loss of biorhythm. Modern diseases like blood pressure, diabetes, skin diseases, insomnia, malignancies and psychological disorders happen due to the loss of biorhythm. Modern houses are responsible for all the diseases mentioned above.

Terraces, french windows facing South and West, toilets in North and East project the house to high thermal torque and solar radiations. Travel of cosmic energy in the house depends upon the position and alignment of the windows/doors. If a door is in the wrong zone, it creates imbalance of the 5 great elements. In modern flats each staircase landing has 2 or 4 entries. Normally, out of these entries 2 are right and 2 are wrong. In all such situations a cosmic correction and elemental remedy becomes necessary.

8.12 Terraces facing South

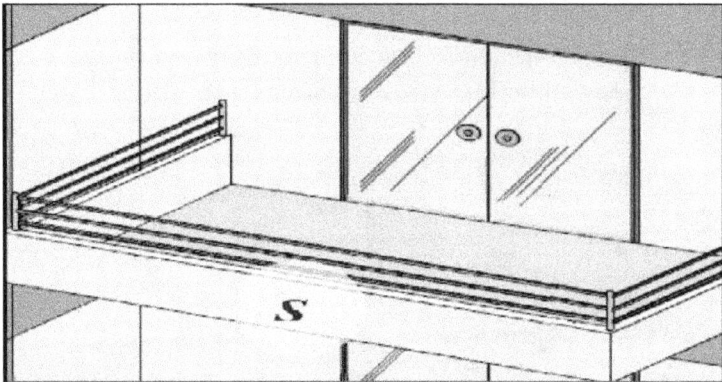

This fault leads to high thermal radiations which disturb the bio-magnetism of the house. This disturbance creates many irregularities in the aspirations. This cosmic fire becomes a weapon against the father staying in the house (i.e. males in the age-range of 30 to 50). Losses in business and defamation in service are allied ill-effects of this asymmetry in the Vaastu.

Remedies

    a) Provide pyramidal canopy in Mangalore tiles to cover the terrace. Pyramid holds, curtails, controls and cuts the streaming of negative energy.

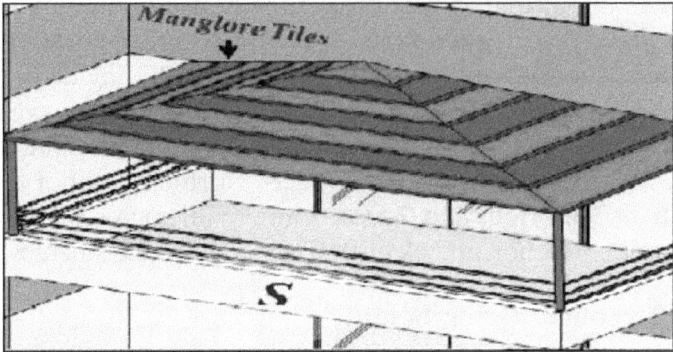

    b) Use Jaisalmer yellow flooring in this zone and keep heavy planters with christmas and almond trees.

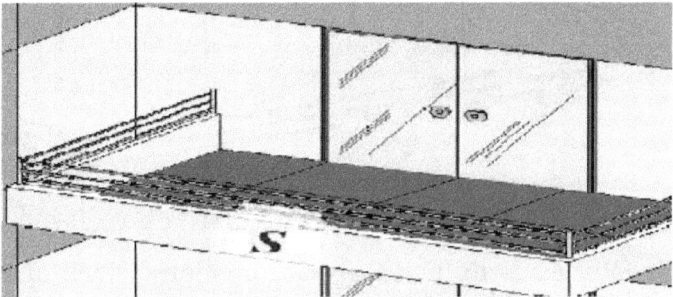

c) Traditional *Tulsi vrindavan* in stone at the center of the terrace cuts the anti-clockwise loops of negative energy.

d) Bury 9 nails of lead weighing 2.5kg each in ascending geometry.

e) Bury 9 blue sapphires at the center of terrace.

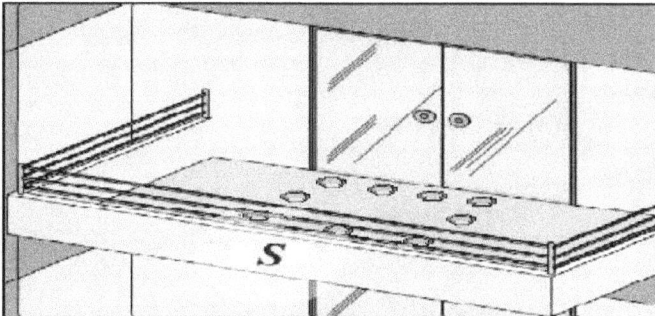

8.13 Terraces facing West

This sink zone represents business partners and life partners. Faults in this zone lead to streaming of subatomic particles which are radioactive and poisonous in nature.

Attack of these particles disturbs the oneness of body and mind. This being the zone of Harshal, a terrace facing West may create all types of eccentricities in behaviour, losses in business due to conflicts with partners, and defeat in court matters.

Remedies

a) Provide pyramidal canopy in white metal or aluminum to cover this terrace zone. Metal being the element of this zone, readjustment in aspiration is possible.

b) Provide Italian blue tiles in this zone.

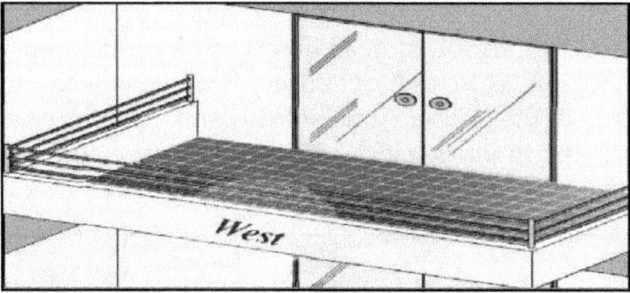

c) Traditional *Tulsi vrindavan* in metal along with a small bonsai of peepal tree in the center of the terrace cuts the anti-clockwise loops of negative energy.

d) Bury 7 nails of lead weighing 1.5kg each in ascending geometry.

8.14 Terraces facing South-East

This is a sink zone which represents 'fire waiting for explosion'. Very often, it is observed that this fault leads to *putranash*, i.e. loss of children. This fault leads to fire hazards in the house. Attack of this sink zone impacts the son staying in the house, leading to arrogance and violence in behaviour.

Remedies

a) Provide pyramidal canopy in wood to cover this terrace zone. Wood, the element of this zone, readjusts the power of fire. In addition, provide a pyramidal cap in copper at the apex point of the pyramid.

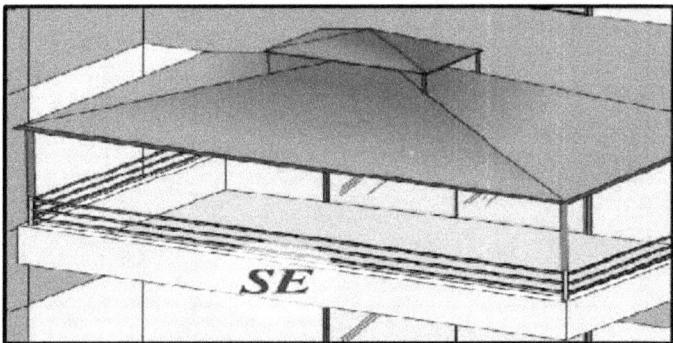

b) Use a combination of white marble and Jaisalmer yellow flooring in this zone.

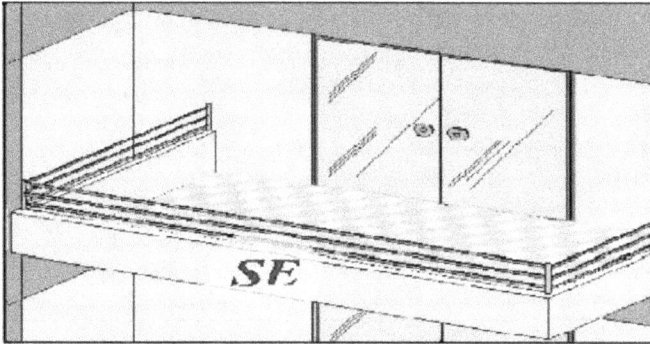

c) Provide a heavy landscape with plantation of golden bamboo and a bonsai of mango tree.

d) Bury copper coins weighing 50gm in each corner of the terrace along with 4 red corals at each corner.

e) Bury 4 yellow sapphires in the center of and above the square of red corals and copper coins.

8.15 Terraces facing South-West

This is the zone of the Earth element and terrace in this zone represents *viparit antral*, i.e. a cosmic void. Imbalance in the Earth element disturbs the entire energy of the house leading to anti-clockwise streaming of the cosmic energy. This situation creates a vortex of devastating forces leading to death, demolition, destruction, defamation and discontinuity at all levels.

Remedies

a) Provide pyramidal canopy in Mangalore tiles to cover the terrace zone. Earth being the element of this zone readjusts the stability of earth.

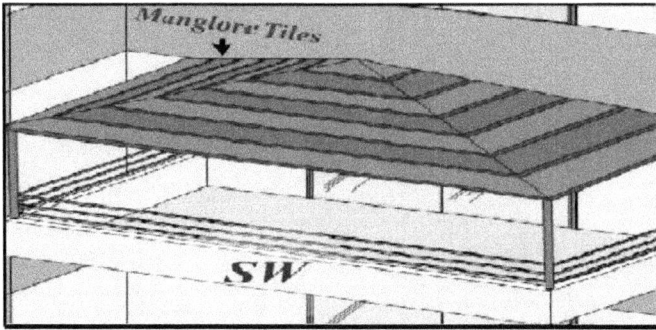

b) Provide Jaisalmer yellow flooring in this zone.

c) Provide a heavy landscape by planting Audumber and almond trees.

d) Traditional *Tulsi vrindavan* in stone at the center of the terrace cuts the anti-clockwise loops of negative energy.

e) Bury 9 nails of lead weighing 2.5kg each in ascending geometry.

f) Bury 9 yellow sapphires in the center of the terrace in square geometry. Place 9 crystals at the center of the square.

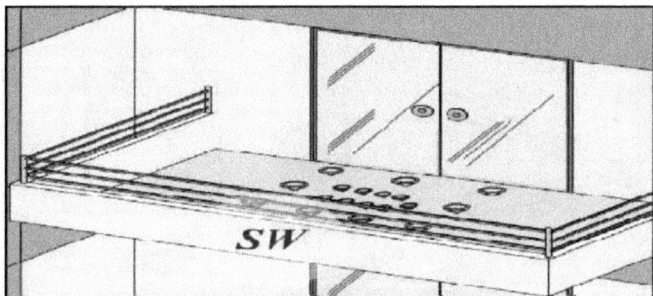

Toilets in wrong zones

Toilets represent blocking of energy, load on aspirations and fragmentation of the deity of *Vaastu Purush Mandal*. It is expected to align the toilets in the sink zones, namely S, SW and W. Toilets in the SE zone disturb the power of Fire element; toilets in N, NE and E zones pollute the divine power of Water element. Toilets in the East zone reduce the power of Aditya, i.e. *pranik* energy. Som, Ish and Aditya are divine deities responsible for peace, prosperity and progress. Toilets in N, NE and E zones reduce the possibility of emergence of these divine deities, leading to all kinds of problems in life. This being the most sacred, divine and passive zone, any fault in this zone acts like slow poisoning.

8.16 Toilets in the North Zone

North zone represents *chandra nadi* (moon streams), i.e. women staying in the house. Flux from the North gives happiness and health to ladies. Toilets in this zone create obstruction for the North flux, leading to problems to ladies, financial losses and worries. Kuber and Som are deities of this zone. All organic processes in the body are governed by the North flux, so they get disturbed due to these toilets. As far as possible, remove the toilets from this zone to avoid the above complications.

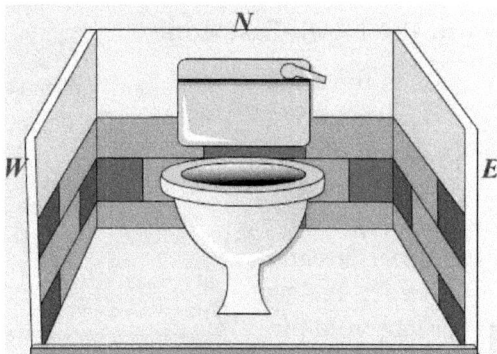

In case removing the toilets from this zone is not possible then:

a) Bury 50gm silver and 27 pearls each at 5 points in a locket form along the perimeter of the toilet.

b) Place white marble around the toilet zone.

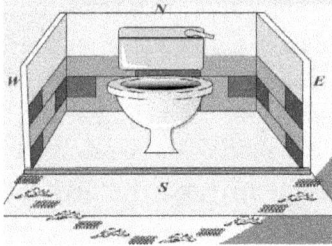

c) Provide mirror panelling on the external surfaces of doors and walls of the toilet.

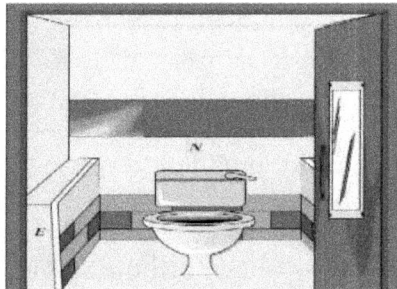

8.17 Toilets in the North-East Zone

North-East zone is the chief source direction representing the confluence of *pranik* and jaivik energy. This is the *Mukh*, i.e. the beginning point of cosmic energies and helix of the energy. Toilets in this zone create voids in

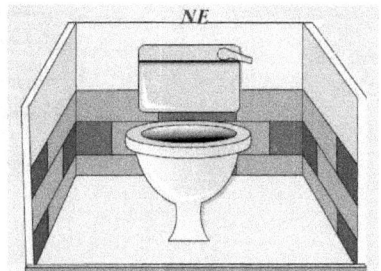

all directions leading to the loss of aspirations. Since the energy does not travel in a *mandalakar* way, there is no possibility of any good happening in this house. As far as possible, remove toilets from this zone to avoid these complications.

If removing the toilets from this zone is not possible then:

a) Bury 50gm silver and 3 crystals each at 8 points in a locket form along the perimeter of the toilet.

b) Place white marble around the toilet zone.

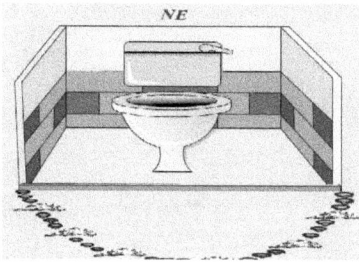

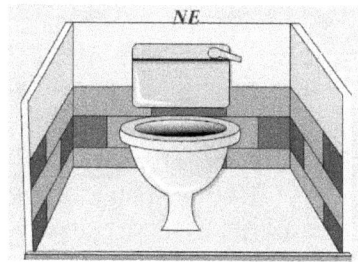

c) Provide mirror panelling on the external surfaces of doors and walls of the toilets.

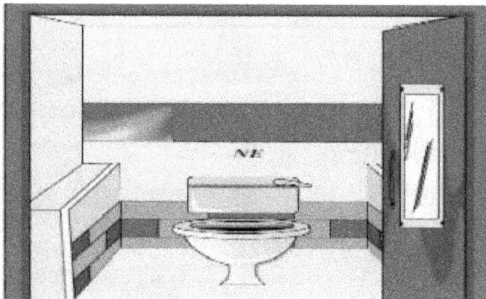

8.18 Toilets in the East Zone

East zone represents Fire in a flame form symbolising order, intelligence, courage and ambition. This is the zone of Sun, Mars and Venus representing intelligence, courage and prosperity respectively. Toilets in this zone create obstruction to success, education and well-being of children. As far as possible, remove toilets from this zone to avoid these complications.

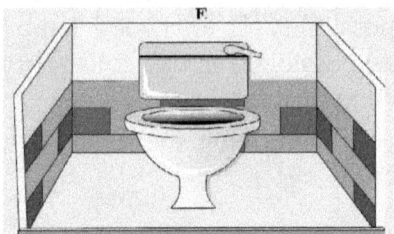

In case removing toilets from this zone is not possible then:

a) Bury 50gm copper and 3 red corals each at 6 points in a locket form along the perimeter of the toilet.

b) Place white marble around the toilet zone.

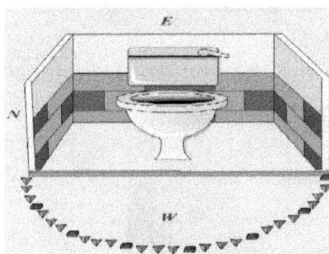

c) Provide deodar wood panelling on the external surfaces of doors and walls of the toilets.

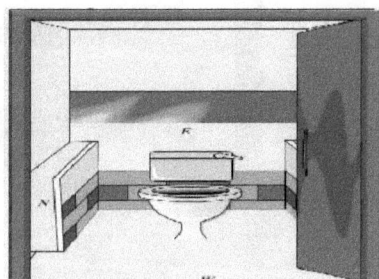

8.19 Toilets in the South-East Zone

South-East zone represents Fire element and is the zone of Mars and Venus. Toilet in this zone disturbs the hormonal cycle of males. Venus and Mars being complimentary planets, disturbed vibration of Venus reduces the courage of Mars. Infertility, cowardice and surrender to circumstances are the main problems due to this fault. As far as possible, remove toilets from this zone to avoid the above complications.

In case removing the toilets from this zone is not possible then:

a) Bury 50gm copper and 3 yellow sapphires each at 5 points in a locket form along the perimeter of the toilet.

b) Place wooden flooring around the toilet zone.

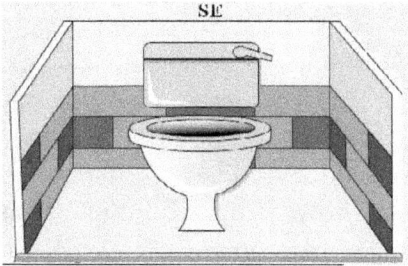

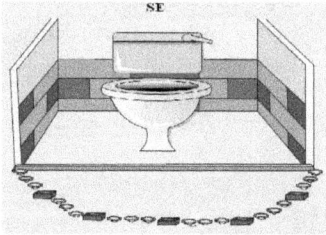

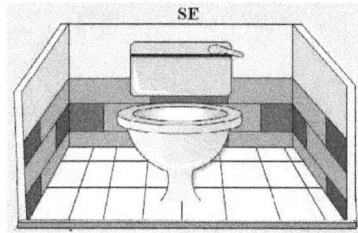

c) Provide deodar wood panelling on the external surfaces of doors and walls of the toilets.

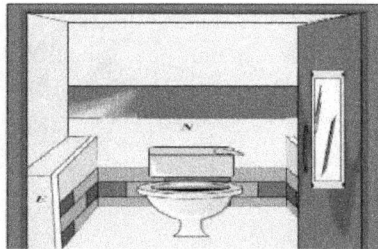

8.20 C-opening in Sink Directions or Ducts in the Sink Zones

When C forms project towards South and West or ducts are in the sink zones then such situations represent *viparit antaral*. This is one of the most complicated situations and is beyond any repair. Staying in such a house is high risk to everybody. Effects are devastating, immediate and horrifying. All haunted houses have this geometry. Hence, the most primary remedial treatment is by way of adjusting the Earth element in areas related to the sink zones. Do not dare to stay in such a house. If removal is not possible then:

a) Provide a deep pyramidal roof over the C shape and limit the activity of *viparit antaral*, i.e. vacuum and void.

b) Bury 100kg lead with 25 blue sapphires at the center of the 'C' opening.

c) Plant 5 Audumber trees at the center of the 'C' opening.

d) Provide a huge yellow stone below the apex of the pyramid as landscape.

8.21 Staircase in the Source Zone (N, NE and E zone)

As far as possible, try to avoid this situation by arranging staircase in the sink zones, i.e. South-East, South, South-West and West. Staircase represents blockage and hindrance to the streaming of energy. It is a heavy load that obstructs the passage of energy. If removal is not possible then:

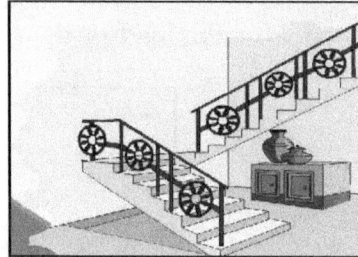

a) Provide white marble and glass for the staircase so that energy streaming is not blocked.

b) If possible, make a wooden staircase.

c) Provide a deep depression in the zone to compensate for the load of the staircase.

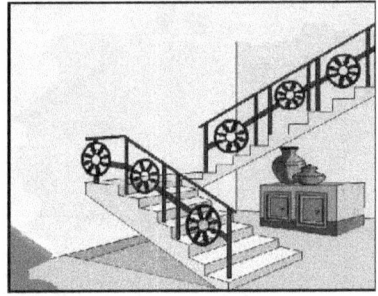

d) Provide a water body in that zone to compensate for the load of the staircase.

9

Case Studies

Let us consider certain case studies in relation to what we have learned in the previous chapters. For that reason, let us try to summarise how the faults act. The following ten faults can be observed in houses which have intense and severe crises. Normally, such houses are on the topmost floor with terrace on top. Toilets are found in the North, North-East, East and South-East zones. Roof slopes are to the South and West directions. North and East, which are the source directions of energy, are found confined and closed. Depressions and borewells in the South, South-West and West zones activate evil forces. House shapes have many cuts and extensions leading to C opening in the South and West zones. Terrace facing the South and West zones lead to severe radiations and imbalance in the thermal equilibrium. Absence of helical *mandalakar* streaming of energy keeps many aspirations and zones in void. Irregular shapes of plots do not help in the proper flowering of virtues of different directions. Hills in the North and East zones accelerate the *pingala* streams of South and West leading to all possible calamities.

9.1 Case Study of Loss of Young Son

Flat on the topmost floor at Karve Nagar, Pune.

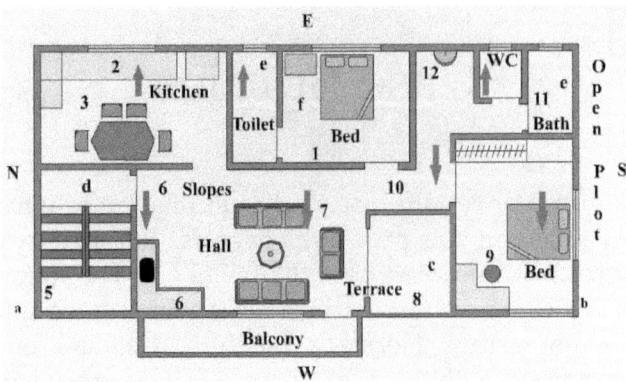

Description

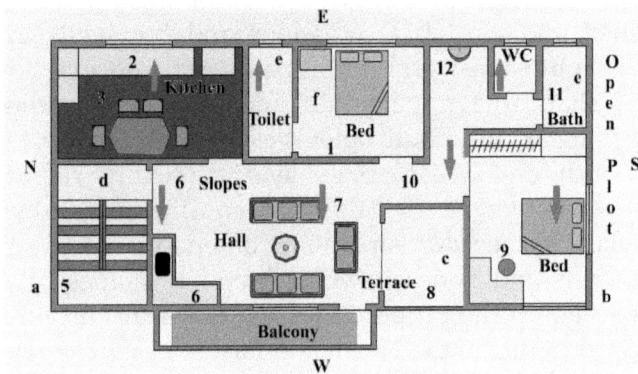

The kitchen and staircase in the North zone have blocked the main energy stream. Astrologically, this zone is represented by the third, fourth and fifth house of the horoscope, which are related to mother and children in the house. Since in this flat the South-East zone is polluted by toilets, i.e. the Water element, reflection related to negativity towards children in the house is hyperactivated, leading to the death of son and grandson.

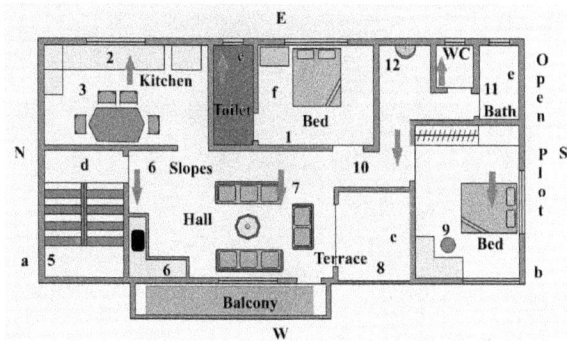

The East zone represents deity Aaditya in *Vaastu Purush Mandal*. Aaditya signifies the Fire element, but it has become weak due to the presence of toilet. East represents cosmic pranik breathing in the house. Here the position of toilet has blocked this source zone.

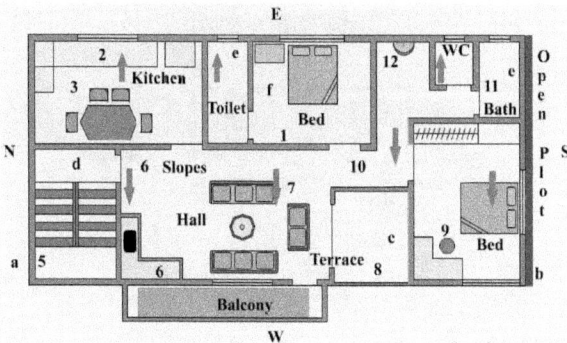

Major roof slopes to the West have projected the entire house to the scorching heat of the Sun and accompanying radiations. This thermal attack has disturbed the bio-magnetism of the house which produces intense negative results of the SW zone. Astrologically, South-West represents the eight and ninth houses and Rahu is the commanding planet of this zone. All activities related to Rahu and the eighth house are severe, intense, extreme and of red shade. In addition, a terrace in the South-West zone and a balcony in the West zone have intensified the negativity.

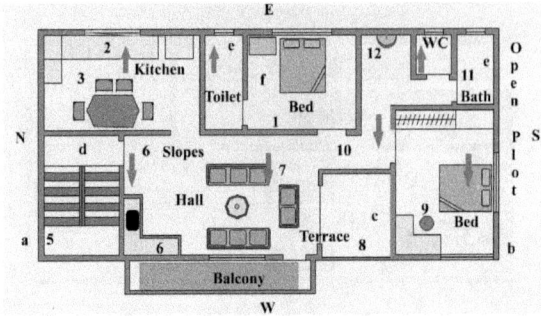

An open plot in the South zone has activated the attack of Yama-pravah leading to all types of failures.

Rectifications

1) Use of yellow stone in the West, South-West and South zones will absorb the *pingala* streams, which in turn will dilute the negative currents.

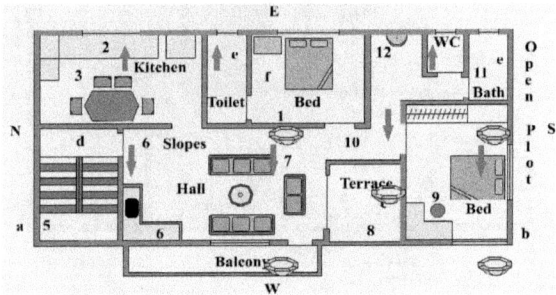

2) A deep pyramidal roof in bamboo over the South-West terrace will eradicate the negativities related to the eigth house and Rahu.

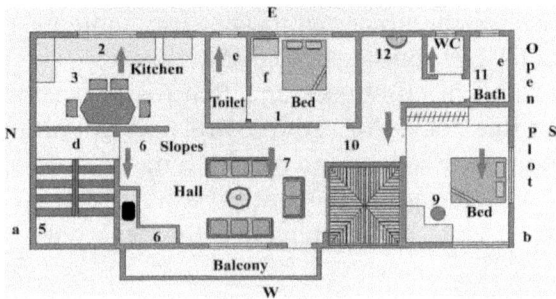

3) A six-foot high parapet wall on the edge of the West side above the roof will control the drooping West slopes of the roof.

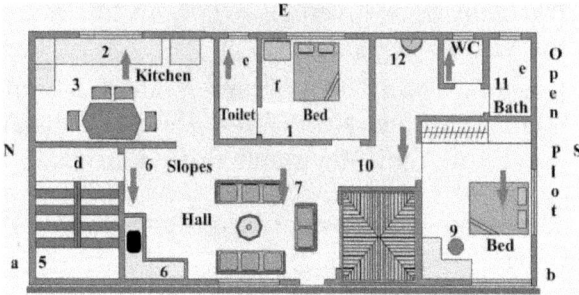

4) Shift the toilet to the South, South-West and West zones so that the Agni tatwa of the South-East will emerge in warmth and happiness.

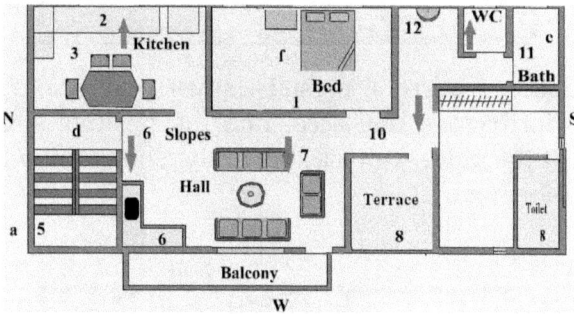

5) More opening in the East side and wooden panelling on the East wall will regulate the *Aaditya* streams of the East zone.

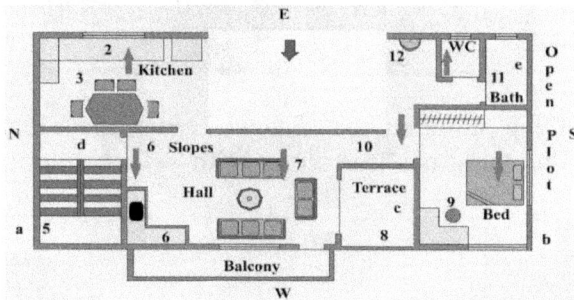

6) Proper placement of auspicious stones as per the *Ratnadhyay* principle will create a *Mandalakar* streaming of cosmic energy.

7) *Dhatudhyay*, as given elsewhere in this book, flares the virtues of planets.

8) Use of *Mantra Beej* pyramids in the South-East, South-West and North-West zones will balance the power of Agni, Vayu and Prithvi tatwa.

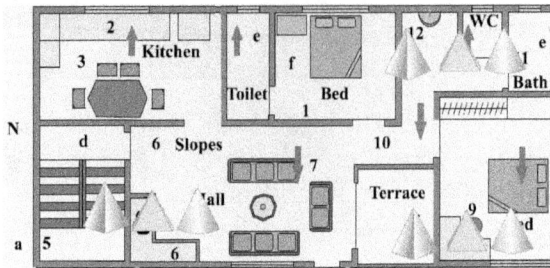

9) Use of mirrors, crystals, silver and pearls in the North zone will accelerate the positive streaming of the deity Som leading to the enhancement of the North zone.

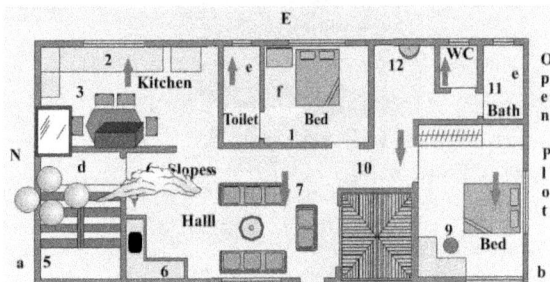

10) Keep stone statues, *Bhoum Yantra* and a bonsai of the christmas tree along with yellow colour in the

South zone. These will reduce the effect of *Yama Pravah* in the house.

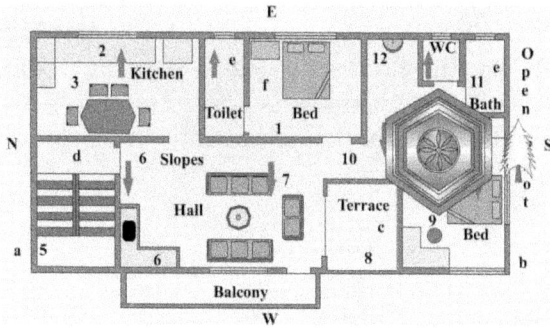

9.2 Case Study of a Premature Death

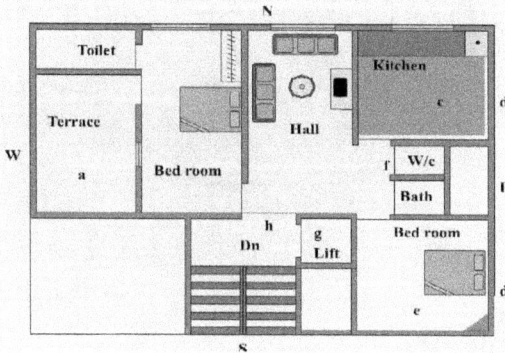

Case Study of a Premature Death

Recently, my friend – a builder and a practicing architect – died at the age of 31. Premature deaths can be explained in terms of Vaastu defects. Traditional Vaastu offers great insights into the profound truths of life and death. If anybody lives in an environment where solar reference is polluted, the five great elements are imbalanced and natural energy streams are blocked, then death, destruction and discontinuity are obvious. This is the foundation of Vaastushastra. Unless two energy streams create a *mandalakar* shape in the house, it is difficult to experience abundance, peace and prosperity.

The example of my friend's house is self-explanatory to prove the tenets of Vaastushastra. As regards the two-stream theory, this house is a failure. As regards the balance of the five great elements, this house is a void. As regards solar reference, this house is a complete black void.

Defects

    a) Flat on the topmost floor.

    b) Terrace in the West and South-West.

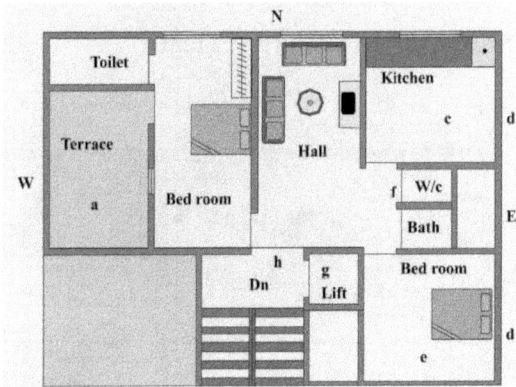

    c) Kitchen in the North-East.

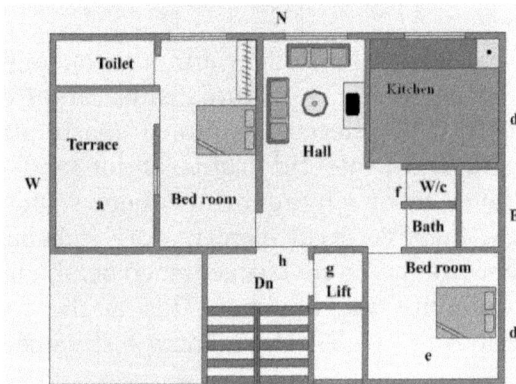

d) East is closed.

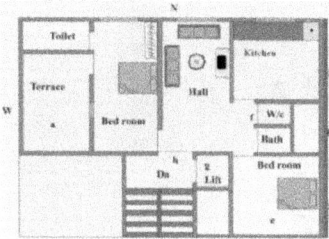

e) Bedroom extension in the South-East.

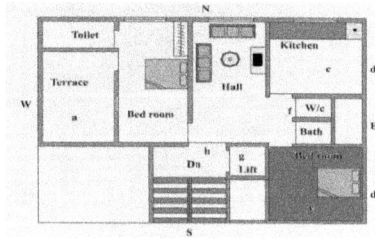

f) Toilets in the central East.

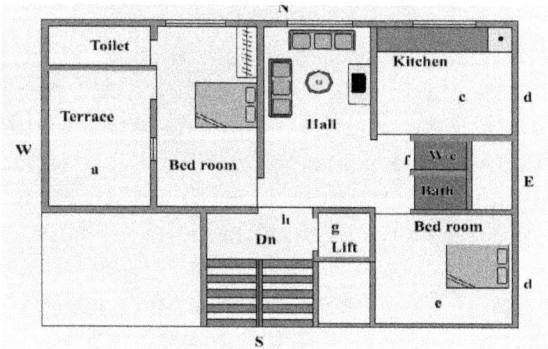

g) Lift well in the South.

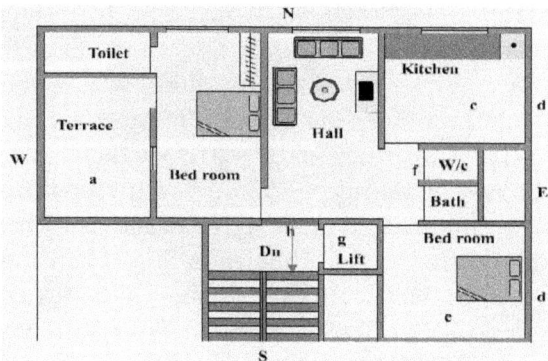

h)   Main door opens where the South zone goes down.

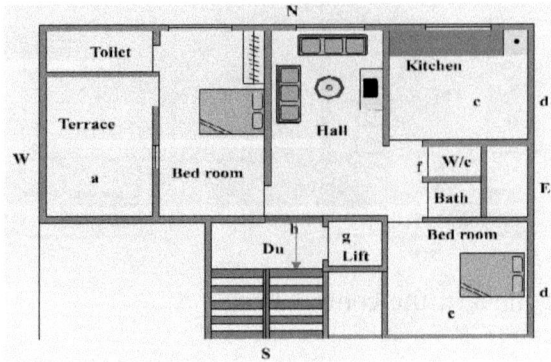

As Vaastushastra is a two-stream theory, so if there is a fault in the East zone along with a fault in the West zone, then the severity of the fault increases. Fault in one direction does not lead to severity unless it is accompanied by a fault in the opposite zone. When two such faults operate together then a negative network of energy disturbs the entire energetics and helical streaming of forces. As can be seen in the above example, there are eight faults which are disturbing this house. Since North and East are source directions of energy, terraces and balconies in these directions are an extension of happiness and prosperity, whereas terraces in the West and South-West directions are extensions of sink directions, which lead to disagreement in every walk of life. The scorching sun disturbs the West side of the terrace, leading to disrupted bio-magnetic networks connected to the house. The uncovered zone of the South-West direction shows loss of the Prithvi tatwa leading to loss of stability. Majority of topmost floor flats with terrace on top experience high thermal disturbance and high temperature torque. This leads to a cut in the helical streaming of positive energy. All such houses experience unfulfilled desire and sorrow. Such flats with East-West length represent intense severity of effects, as the projection to the West leads to high levels of exposure of the living spaces to the scorching sun.

The East is closed. Such a situation blocks the cosmic *aaditya* streams. This leads to a situation similar to the one where the soul of the house is missing. This is what has happened after the death of the head of the family in this house. Progress, promotion and purity are the contributions of the East *aaditya* streams. A closed East and an open West together lead to severe effects. Extensions in the South-East are extensions of the fire zone. This situation further adds to the disturbance in the thermal balance of the house which effects the elemental balance also. A bedroom, particularly, in this extended South-East zone is a mahadosha, i.e. severe fault. Kitchen not being in this zone and bedroom being in this zone leads to multiplication of faults.

The East zone is marked for fire with the quality of warmth. This warmth is necessary to keep the various hormones and secretions in the cosmic body of a human being in balance. A toilet in this zone is viparit to the *aaditya* streams. East represents self, personality and nature. In modern constructions, lift well represents a depression. When such depressions fall in the South, South-West and West zones, they activate the sink zones leading to a high possibility of premature death and discontinuity.

The South zone represents father in the house, so any fault in the South zone attacks the father in the house, which is exactly what has happened in this case. This severe fault in the South is accompanied with another entrance fault in the South zone. Multiple faults in the zone create an intense negativity towards the occupant of the space.

The only positive area of the house is the large opening in the North zone, which has kept the financial condition of the house in a stable position.

Rectification

1) A pyramidal roof of towering height in the South-West zone will readjust the energies of the house. If a small rock garden is planned in this zone then the lost rhythm of the Prithvi tatwa can be recalled, leading to stability and balance. Use yellow raised flooring in this zone.

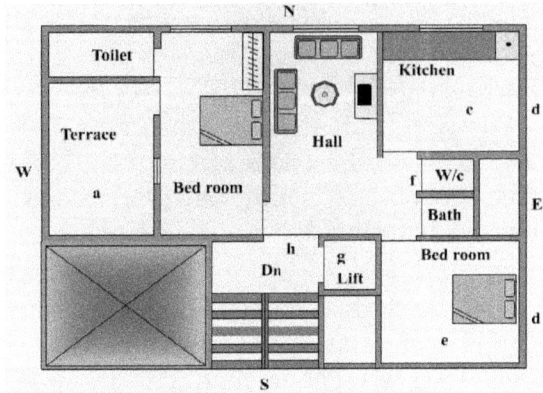

2) Provide a blue shed with transparent sheets in the West zone with slope to the North side. Blue colour is symbolic of Saturn and the Wind element, leading to the helical streaming of energy.

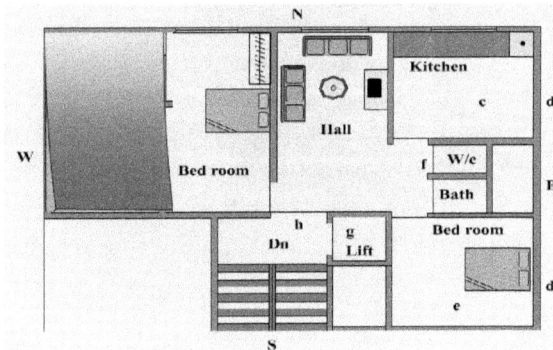

3) Bury 3 blue sapphires in the West zone along with one yellow sapphire in the South-West zone of the terrace to readjust the bio-rhythm.

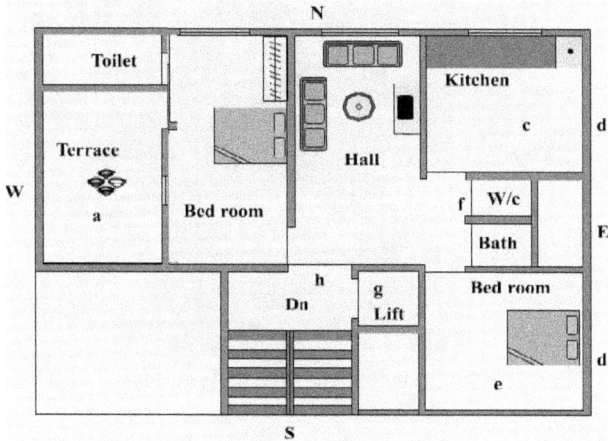

4) Provide 9 pyramids in the South entrance ceiling and paint them in gold. Use Jaisalmer yellow stone flooring on the staircase landing zone. Bury 5kg lead in this landing zone. The assembly of Jaisalmer yellow flooring, golden pyramidal roof and lead metal will curtail the activity of South streams.

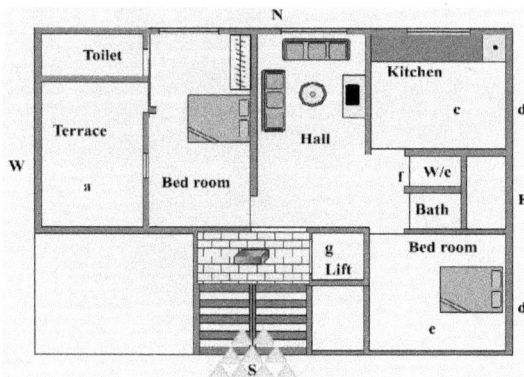

5) Bury 3 triangular red corals along the toilets in the East zone to reduce the water-effect of the toilet.

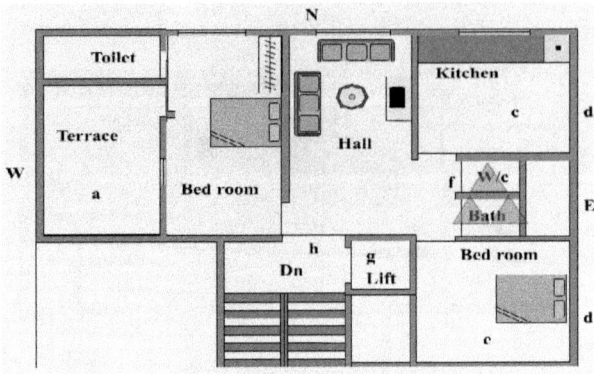

6) Shift the kitchen to the South-East zone and readjust the bedroom in the North-East zone.

7) Standard procedures of *Ratnadhyay, Dhatuadhyay* and forms/pyramids are powerful remedies to balance the 5 great elements, to create the cosmic aura of the 9 planets and to stream the energy in a *mandalakar* way.

8) Mirrors, crystals, wooden panelling, stone claddings, level differences, limiting ventilations are also powerful tools to energise the living spaces.

Important Charts/Maps/ Figures

Colour scheme based on directions and planets

Direction	Planet	Colour
East	Sun	Bright white
North-East	Jupiter	Golden yellow
North	Mercury	Green
North-West	Moon	White
West	Saturn	Blue
South-West	Rahu	Green
South	Mars	Red, Pink
South-East	Venus	Silver white

Zoning of Industrial Activities

In an industrial undertaking multiple activities take place simultaneously. To achieve better co-ordination and cohesion in these activities, it is desirable that specific operations are restricted to definite zones on the basis of involved energy levels.

Activity	Zone
Research and development	North-East
Heavy loads and activity	South-West
Thermal activity	South-East
Finished products	North-West
Accounts and legal activity	East
Chief Executive's cabin	South-West (South side)
Toilet/Canteen/Retiring Room	West

Landscape Details

To achieve harmony with nature and bliss in the surrounding environment, it is essential that a definite shape is given to the plot and it is aligned properly with the geo-magnetic axis. For the plot under study, the following measures are recommended as per *Vaastushastra*:

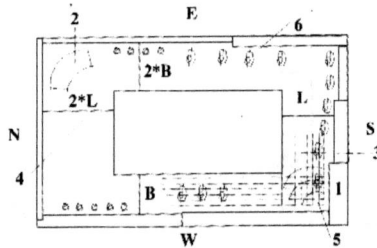

Sketch and Landscape Details of the Industrial Plot

1. Build a heavy compound wall 24" thick and 7' high in the South-West zone, gradually reducing it to 18" thick and 5' high in the South-East side, and 9" thick and 3' high in the North and East sides. To match the shape, size and periphery of 'Vaastu-kshetra' with the helix pattern, these varying compound wall depths, widths and heights are very useful. The helical alignment of compound wall balances

the vices and virtues related to Vaastu directions and sub-directions.

2. Provide a marble finish lunar-shaped water pool in the North-East corner, having outer perimeter of 20ft, inner perimeter of 15ft, and depth 5ft. A circular water body with diameter 8ft and depth 3ft can also be used. The exposed water surface in the North-East polarises the solar rays in transverse direction creating a source of ordered *jaivik* energy.

3. Fill the pits in the West, South-West and South zones to attain ground slopes towards the North and East. This procedure offsets energy-matter imbalance on account of heavy stress concentration in the South-West zone. Elevating the South-West zone in a Vaastu-kshetra reorients the cosmic energy flow to simulate a cosmic energy helix in the environment.

4. The North and the East side margins should be twice as much as those of the South and the West.

5. Provide heavy *gurutwa* pedestal load in the South-West corner of the plot. The aligned geo-magnetic fields of a Vaastu are disturbed due to high thermal activity in the South-West zone. The disturbed energy field can be balanced with heavy loads in this zone.

6. Main buildings should be placed in the South-West zone and aligned in such a manner that the North-South axis of the building should match the geo-magnetic axis. The shape of the building should be rectangular.

7. Borewell should be provided in the North-East corner.

8. Septic tank should be located in the North-West zone.

9. Provide pyramid-like structures made of organic matter like bamboo or wood over South-West passages. The dimensions of the pyramid could be 8ft x 8ft x 3ft.

Application of Shatpad Vaastu, Ekashitipad Vaastu, and Chatushashtipad Vaastu Concepts

Vaastu-Purush-Mandal	Matrix	Vaastu Type
Chatushashtipad	8 X 8	Housing colony layouts, planning of small townships, government or military camps, etc.
Ekashitipad	9 X 9	Houses for different classes of the society, palaces, public places, government offices, etc.
Shatpad	10 X 10	Tall buildings, mansions, temples, auditoriums, etc.

NAG SHOSH	NAG	MUKH YA	BHAL LAT	SOM	CHA RAK	ADITI	ADITI PARJ ANYA
SHOSH	RUD RA	MUKH YA	BHAL LAT	SOM	CHA RAK	APA VAT SA	PARJ ANYA
ASUR	ASUR	YAKS HMA	PRIT HVI	DHA R	AAP	JAYA NTA	JAYA NTA
JALES HWAR	JALES HWAR	MIT RA	BRAH MA	BRAH MA	ARY	MAHE NDRA	MAHE NDRA
PUSH PADA NTA	PUSH PADA NTA	MIT RA	BRAH MA	BRAH MA	AMA	RAVI	RAVI
SUJ RIVA	SUJ RIVA	JAYA	VI SW	VA AN	SAVI TRU	SAT YA	SAT YA
DOUV ARIK	INDRA	GAN DHA RVA	YAMA	GRAIH KSHA TA	VITA THA	SAVI TRU	BHRU SHA
DOUV ARIK BHRU NGA	BHRU NGA RAJ	GAN DHA RVA	YAMA	GRAIH KSHA TA	VITA THA	POO SHA	BHRU SHA POO SHA

SOUTH

Chatushashtipad Vaastu Matrix of 8 X 8 squares

Vaastu Purush Mandal with 8 x 8 = 64 squares is useful for planning colony layouts and smaller townships.

ROG	NAG	MUKH YA	BHAL LAT	SOM	CHA RAK	ADITI	DITI	SHI KHI
PAPA YAKS HMA	RUD RA	MUKH YA	**PRIT HVI DHAR**	**PRIT HVI DHAR**	**PRIT HVI DHAR**	ADITI	AAP	PARJ ANYA
SHOSH	SHOSH	RUD RA JAYA	**PRIT HVI DHAR**	**PRIT HVI DHAR**	**PRIT HVI DHAR**	APP VATSA	JAYA NTA	JAYA NTA
ASUR	**MIT RA**	**MIT RA**	BRAH MA	BRAH MA	BRAH MA	**ARY MA**	**ARY MA**	MAHE NDRA
VARU NA	**MIT RA**	**MIT RA**	BRAH MA	BRAH MA	BRAH MA	**ARY MA**	**ARY MA**	RAVI
PUSH PADA NTA	**MIT RA**	**MIT RA**	BRAH MA	BRAH MA	BRAH MA	**ARY MA**	**ARY MA**	SAT YA
SUG RIVA	SUG RIVA	INDRA JAYA	**VIVA SWAN**	**VIVA SWAN**	**VIVA SWAN**	SAVI TRU	BHRU SHA	BHRU SHA
DOUV ARIK	INDRA	GAN DHA RVA	**VIVA SWAN**	**VIVA SWAN**	**VIVA SWAN**	VITA THA	SAVI TRU	NAB HA
PUT RA	MRI GA	BHRU NGA RAJ	GAN DHA RVA	YAMA	GRAIH KSHA TA	VITA THA	POO SHA	ANIL

Ekashitipad Vaastu Matrix of 9 X 9 squares

Vaastu Purush Mandal with 9 x 9 = 81 squares is used in planning houses.

Marmasthan

North

ROG / MUK HYA   ADITI   HUTA SHAN   dal

SHO SH   JAY ANT

WEST   EAST

SUG RIVA   BRH USH   SHI RA

PIT RU   MRI GA   VITI THTA   VAYU

SOUTH

VANSH

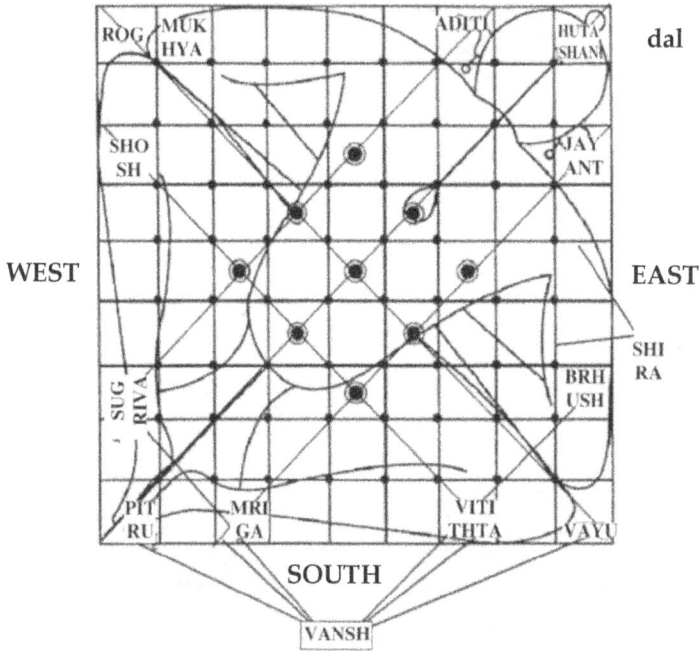

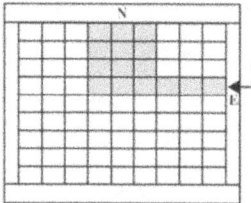

a : Habitation zone for intellectuals

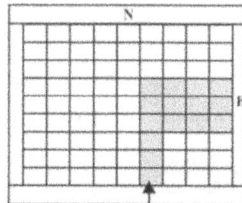

b : Habitation zone for military/police

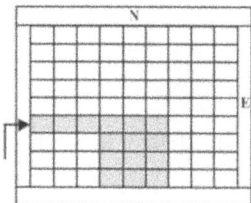

c : Habitation zone for traders

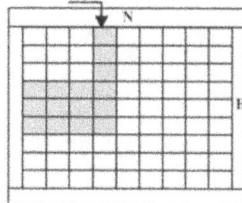

d : Habitation zone for the working-class

श्रियं दाहं तथा मृत्युं धनहानिं सुतक्षयम्।
प्रवासं धनलाभं च विद्यालाभं क्रमेण च।
विदध्यार चिरेणैव पूर्वदिप्लववतो मही।
मध्यप्लवा मही नेष्टा न शुभाप्लवतत्परा॥

(बृहद् वास्तुमाला)

Here, gradients in various directions of a plot are correlated with different facets of human life:

Land sloping towards	Quality indicated
East	prosperity
South-East	burning sensation
South	advent of death
South-West	loss of wealth
West	loss of offspring
North-West	instability
North	prosperity
North-East	good education
Land hollow at centre	hardship in life

Horoscope Projection in North-Indian Style

Effect of Various Houses in a Horoscope

House No.	Parameters influenced by specific houses in the horoscope
1.	personality, nature, likes/dislikes, head, face, height, skin, colour, hair, rajayoga
2.	facial expressions, family, expenses, ancestral property, shares, knowledge
3.	relatives, brotherhood, travel, voice, music, literature, reading, writing, bravery, mental illness, will power
4.	spouse, close friends, pet animals, material benefits, vehicle, vaastu, agriculture, business know-how, aesthetics, flowers and fragrance, water-related items, chest, higher education, degrees, godliness
5.	education, degree, learning, culture, love, marriage, devotion, dreams, artist, art, entertainment, theatre, racing, gambling
6.	enemies, problems in life, sorrow, company, job, civil servant, stomach, digestive system
7.	spouse, partnership, sexual life, kidney, married life, divorce, competitors, entertainment, art, court matters, war
8.	death, difficulties, accidents, ancestral rights, dowry, corruption, illegal gains, godliness
9.	religion, vision, higher education, temple, philosophy, progress, guru/guide, judge, court matters, travel
10.	prestige, fame, promotion, rights, paternal backing business, job, head, sleeplessness, social and political life, rajayoga
11.	gains, jewellery, fashion, clothes, circle of friends, returns, left ear
12.	loss of property, financial crisis, penalty, punishment, feet, moksha, sanyas, godliness

□ Square   **Prithvi tatwa (Earth)**

⌂ Half-circle   **Jal tatwa (Water)**

△ Triangle   **Agni tatwa (Fire)**

○ Circle   **Vayu tatwa (Wind)**

Shapes of the Five Great Elements

111

Virtues and qualities of N/S/E/W.

EAST

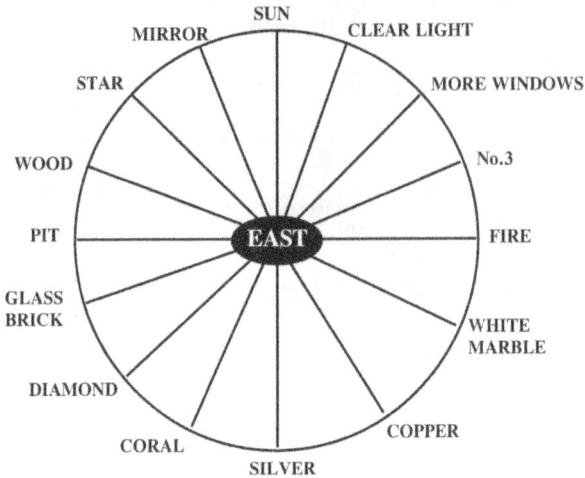

WEST

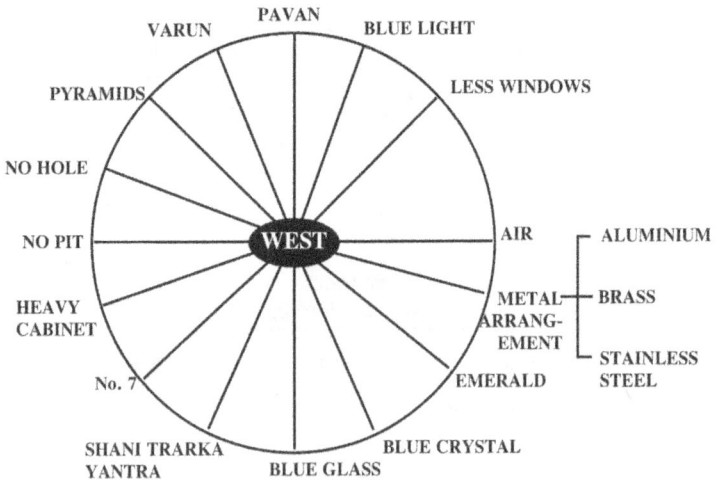

SOUTH

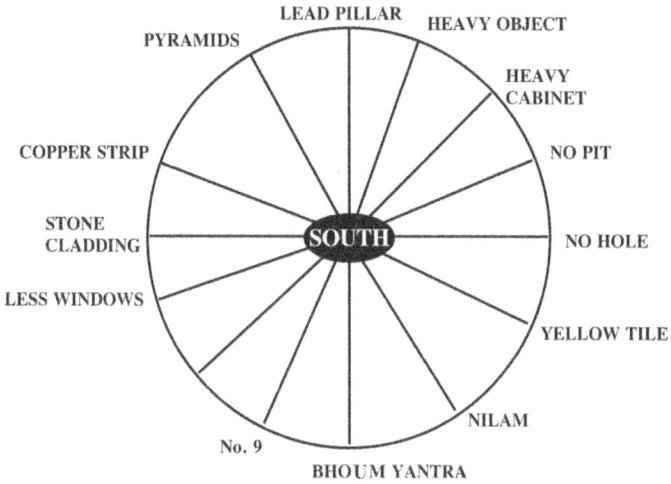

SOUTH

- LEAD PILLAR
- HEAVY OBJECT
- PYRAMIDS
- HEAVY CABINET
- COPPER STRIP
- NO PIT
- STONE CLADDING
- NO HOLE
- LESS WINDOWS
- YELLOW TILE
- No. 9
- NILAM
- BHOUM YANTRA

NORTH

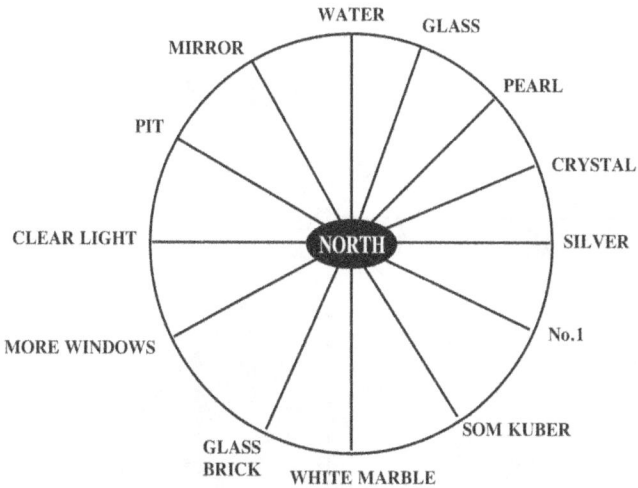

NORTH

- WATER
- GLASS
- MIRROR
- PEARL
- PIT
- CRYSTAL
- CLEAR LIGHT
- SILVER
- MORE WINDOWS
- No.1
- GLASS BRICK
- SOM KUBER
- WHITE MARBLE

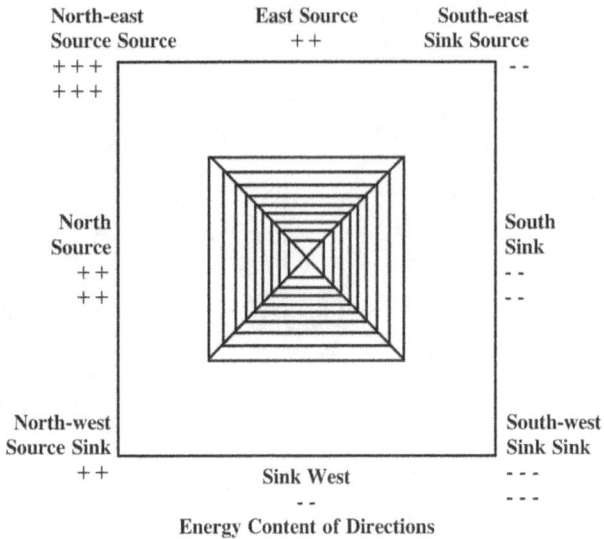

North-east Source Source +++ +++	East Source ++	South-east Sink Source --
North Source ++ ++		South Sink -- --
North-west Source Sink ++	Sink West --	South-west Sink Sink --- ---

Energy Content of Directions

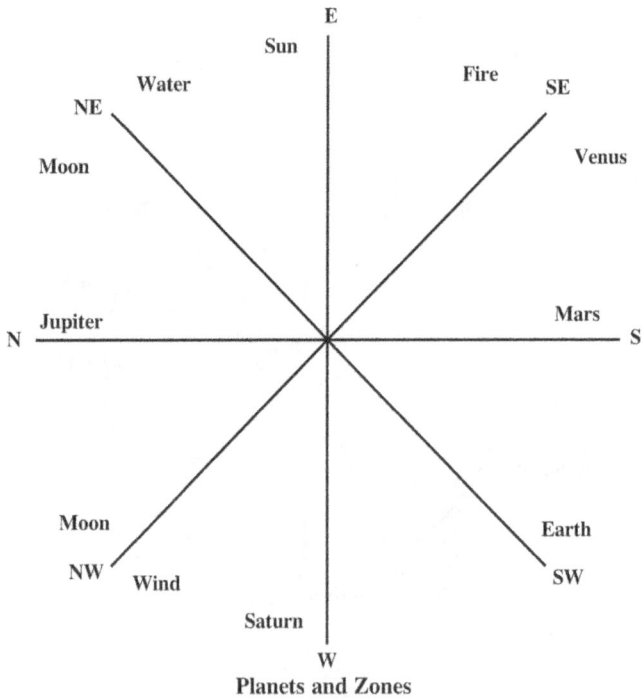

Planets and Zones

114

Tatwa	Element	Moon Sign	Colour	Enemy	Friend	Best Friend
Jal	Water	Cancer, Pisces, Scorpio	White	Agni	Vayu	Prithvi
Prithvi	Earth	Taurus, Virgo, Capricorn	Yellow	Vayu	Agni	Jal
Agni	Fire	Aries, Leo, Sagittarius	Red	Jal	Prithvi	Vayu
Vayu	Wind	Gemini, Libra Aquarius	Blue	Prithvi	Jal	Agni

Interrelationship of Elements

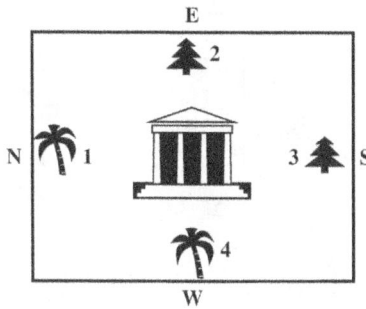

1. Plaksha-ficus infectoria   2. Banyan Tree
3. Audumbar Tree   4. Peepal Tree

Plot and Plants

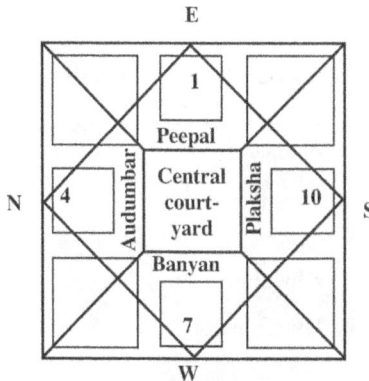

Directions-Zones-Plants

115

Use of Metals

S. no.	Metals	Descendent	Day	Direction
1.	Zinc	Jupiter	Thursday	North
2.	Copper	Mars	Tuesday	East
3.	Bronze	Mercury	Wednesday	West
4.	Lead	Saturn	Saturday	South

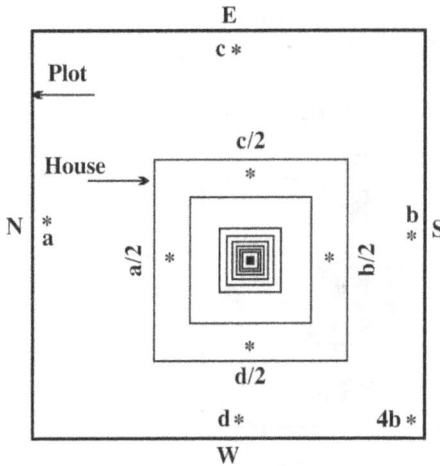

a - 100 gm Zinc

b - 800 gm Lead

c - 200 gm Copper

d - 400 gm Bronze

4b - 3200 gm lead

Dhatuadhyay

Nomenclature of Trishala

Trishala with	Name	Effect
Eastern Sala	Sukshetra	Prosperity
Southern Sala	Culli	Loss of wealth
Western Sala	Dhwamsa	Loss of children; enmity
Northern Sala	Hiranyanabh	Wealth

N

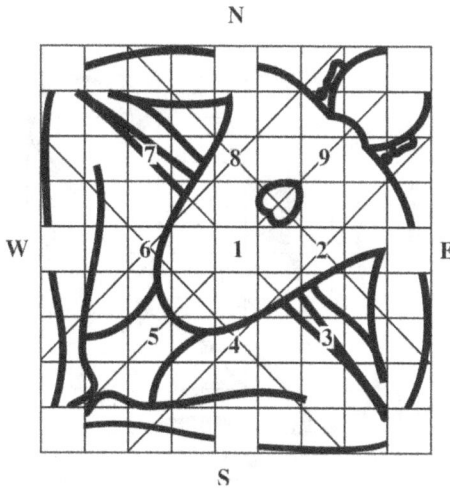

W   E

S

Ratnadhyay for Buildings or Bungalows

The following mantras should be recited 108 times while placing plates on unhusked rice with the below mentioned ratnas at given points:

Stones, Planets and Mantras

S. no	Stones	Planet	Mantra
1.	Ruby	Sun	OM rham rhim rhoum sah: suryay namah.
2.	Red Coral	Mars	OM kram krim kroum sah: bhoumaya namah.
3.	Yellow Sapphire	Jupiter	OM gram grim ghroum sah: gurave namah.
4.	Cat's eye	Ketu	OM shram shrim shroum sah: ketve namah.
5.	Crystal	Venus	OM dhram dhrim dhroum sah: shukraya namah.
6.	Neelam	Saturn	OM pram prim proum sah: shanishcharay namah.
7.	Neelam	Saturn	OM pram prim proum sah: shanishcharay namah.
8.	Green Emerald	Mercury	OM bram brim broum sah: budhay namah.
9.	Pearl	Moon	OM shram shrim shroum sah: somaya namah.

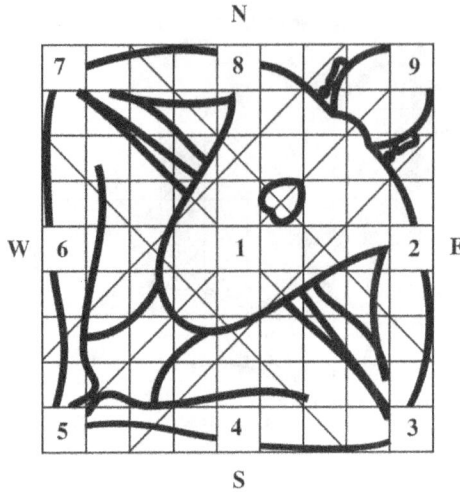

Ratnadhyay for Plot

The following mantras should be recited 108 times while placing plates on unhusked rice with the below mentioned ratnas at given points:

Stones, Planets and Mantras

S. no. Stones	Planet	Mantra
1. Ruby	Sun	OM rham rhim rhoum sah: suryay namah.
2. Red Coral	Mars	OM kram krim kroum sah: bhoumaya namah.
3. Crystal	Venus	OM dhram dhrim dhroum sah: shukraya namah.
4. Neelam	Saturn	OM pram prim proum sah: shanishcharay namah.
5. Yellow Sapphire	Jupiter	OM gram grim ghroum sah: gurave namah.
6. Green Emerald	Mercury	OM bram brim broum sah: budhay namah.
7. Gomed	Rahu	OM bhram bhrim bhroum sah: rahve namah.
8. Pearl	Moon	OM shram shrim shroum sah: somaya namah.
9. Sphatika	Shiv	Mahamrutyunjay mantra.

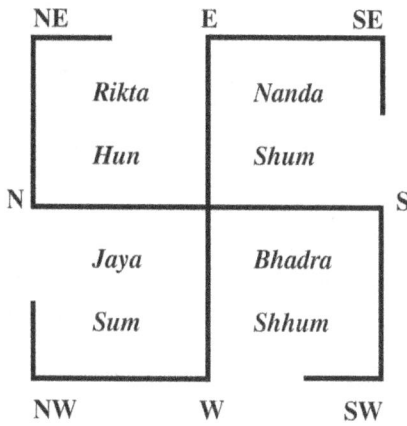

Swastika

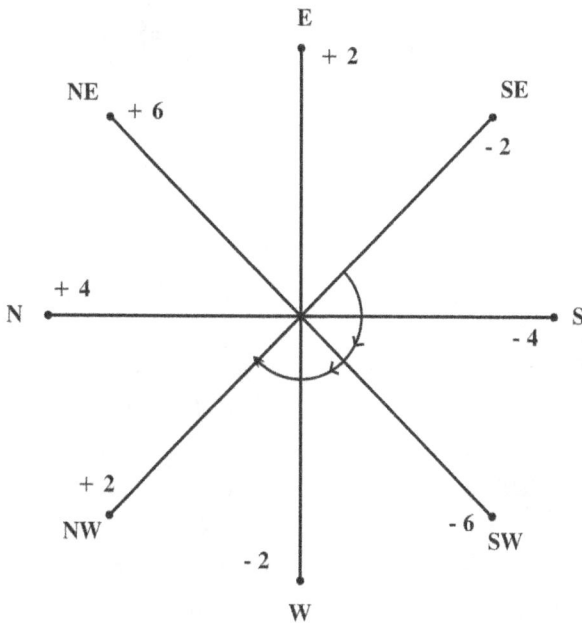

Directions and Energy Count

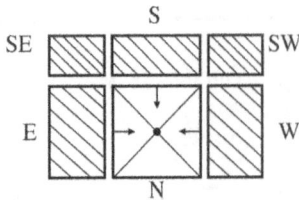

Hiranyanabham
Uttar-choolha

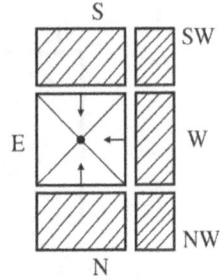

Sukshetram
Poorva-choolha

'C' Opening in North and East (Source *Choolha*)

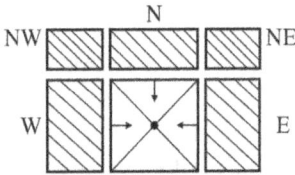

Sulam
Dakshin-choolha

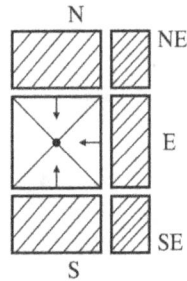

Paksaghnam
Pashchim-choolha

'C' Opening in South and West (Sink *Choolha*)

S.No.	Divshala with	Name	Effect
1.	Southern and Northern	Kaca	Quarrel and fear
2.	Western and Eastern	Siddhartha	Acquisition of wealth
3.	Western and Northern	Yamasurpa	Death
4.	Northern and Eastern	Danda	Fear, misery
5.	Eastern and Southern	Vata	Quarrel
6.	Southern and Western	Siddhartha	Acquisition of wealth

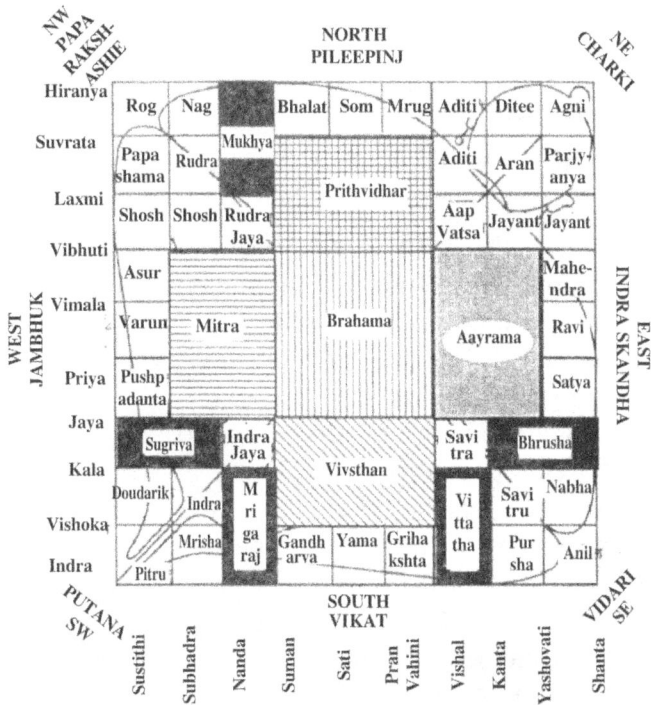

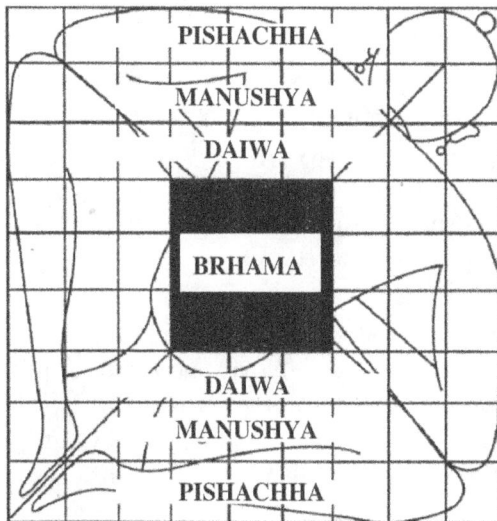

Important Notes

1. Bury 500gm cultured pearls and 35gm silver in the North of the house to enhance the North aspirations. This will give peace and cooling effect to the house along with financial growth.

2. Use white marble in the North zone so that *jaivik oorja* (organic streams) gets reinforced, leading to the good health of females, sound sleep of males and better options in life.

3. Use crystal chandelier in the North zone to reinforce the virtues of the source zones leading to general wish-fulfillment.

4. North represents the fourth house in horoscope, the Water element, the ladies in the house, prosperity of the house, and the rhythm of hormones in ladies. Toilet or staircase in the North disturbs the cycle of hormones in ladies leading to malignancy, breast cancer and allergies.

5. Skylight from the North roof excites the vibration of the deity Som leading to peace, prosperity and progress. This skylight forces energy to travel in a *mandalakar* path leading to the flowering of aspirations of all directions; so in a bungalow or in the topmost floor flat create a hole by core cutting in a slab.

6. To make the slope of land towards North, provide deep bores in the North zone in a lunar form. Depression in the North excites the North streams and strengthens the North deities. Lunar form gives cosmic power to the Water element.

7. Provide 5'x 5'x 5' depression in the North zone of the plinth. Provide white marble to all six sides of this pit. Bury 500gm of pearls in the pit. Depressed earth in the North zone gives virtue to the Water element. Moon streams from the depressed North assure success and fulfillment of wishes.

8. Lunar-shaped water body in the North zone with depression, white marble finish and crystals with water give divine touch to the deities of North i.e. Soma and Kuber. It showers prosperity and strength to enjoy it.

9. Bury 8 *sphatik Lingam* in a crescent form along with rice grains, camphor and sandalwood paste in the North-East zone. This adds virtue to deity Shikhi leading to the transformation of water elements into *Teertha* (Divine water).

10. Bury 500gm of pearls with 35gm silver in the *Aap-Aapvatsa* zone of the North-East. This strengthens the cosmic power of the Water element which gives helical *pranavakar* path to light and energy. It assures divine support in every form of life.

11. Provide white marble in NE zone so that stream of photons, i.e ray of light gets polarised, which in turn helps to create the continuum where mind, body and intellect get unified. Fire emerges as a divine form that ignites many dimensional flames.

12. Make holes in the ceiling to get skylight from the North-East zone. A direct light, i.e. Chi gives an auspicious form to deity Shikhi which is situated in the crest of Vaastu Purusha. It is the place where vibration of Shiva transforms everything into *Satyam, Shivam and Sundaram.*

13. Provide borewells in the *Aap-Aapvatsa* zone of the North-East. This equalises all the faults related to land, gradients and slopes. Automatically the

inverted fountain of cosmic energy fulfils the aspiration of all directions, leading to a powerful Angdevta. Powerful Angdevta protects the Vaastu from encroaching negative energy.

14. Never make an underground water tank or borewell in the exact NE corner. In this corner a divine fire form called *Shikhi* gets disturbed due to this water element. Such depressed fire is called *viprit agni* which leads to loss of intelligence and moral values.

15. Keep 1 silver pot filled with pearls and a crystal at the centre of the North-East zone. Pearls give grace to deity *Aap-Aapvatsa*, crystal gives polarised aura to deity *Shikhi*. A mirror panelling around this assembly enhances the aspirations of the North zone. Such enhancement of the main source direction means fulfillment of purpose, completeness of form and contentment for the person.

16. Water element in the North is a sign of prosperity whereas Water element in the North-East is a divine crystal form. Unless deities of both zones get proper vibrations, helical *purnbahu* streaming of cosmic energy is impossible. When *satvik* (divine) and *rajsik* (royal) work together then order and discipline are ensured.

17. Bury 50gm copper coins each at 6 apex points of a star and 50gm silver at the centre of the central East zone. Mars represents copper and Moon represents silver. Confluence of Mars and Moon gives courage and prosperity, traditionally called *Dhairya-Laxmi*.

18. Banyan tree in the East zone without its shadow falling on the house or a small bonsai of banyan tree in the East zone of the house blesses the longevity of the occupants. Courage, success and intergrity are showered due to the bio-rhythm shared with this tree from the East zone.

19. *Indra, Ravi, Satya,* i.e. success, light and morals are the deities of East. If criminals and politicians get the vibration of East, the darkness of their mind will get wiped out. High moral values and integrity are the aura of East. Education, intelligence and courage are the root aspirations of this zone.

20. East represents positive form of fire, i.e. flame. Flame or star is considered a divine medium to get connected to a god or mother nature. Fire in the East is a positive desire related to creation and continuity. Houses without East vibrations may have only daughters or no children at all.

21. If East is closed then provide a cosmic window in East, i.e. a combination of wooden panelling, copper and silver inlay, red corals and crystals. Use mirrors, white marble and chandelier in the East. East aspirations get enhanced by this assembly in the East zone.

22. If East is closed then drink water from a copper pot or water boiled with gold coins, do *bhasrika pranayam* and a prolonged japa of *'rhim'*. This will excite the cosmic fire in the 5 shields of your consciousness.

23. Faults in East have predominant effect on the males of the house. Sun, Mars and Venus get affected in your body if the East vibration is polluted. Rhythm is given by North, synchronicity is given by East and frequency is attained by North-East.

24. Toilets, staircase, raised levels, less site margin and heavy plantation are the severe faults of North, North-East and East zones. Sound and light are the attributes of these source directions so if their vibration is disturbed, it leads to noise and darkness in life.

25. South-East represents intense, monstrous form of fire – explosion. Hence, fire from South-East zone

needs to be controlled. Even a tree with red flowers is not allowed in this zone. Controlled fire, controlled South-East zone gives warmth to the house.

26. Explosive, intense fire represent thirst, hunger and sensuous desire, which is classified with the South-East zone. Crimes begin with this zone if its vibration is disturbed. Four divisions near Brahma are cosmic deities viz. Savita and Savitru.

27. Four divisions near Brahmas are reserved for the bedroom of young growing sons in the house. They share the ascending attitude, courage and purity of deities Savita and Savitru. The bed should be with head to the East and legs to the West. Study table should face North with a closed and confined South.

28. Terrace facing South-East or a cut in the South-East or well in the South-East represents depressed fire which results in infertility or low sperm count in males. It is mandatory to use pyramidal roof over terraces, bury 2.5 kg copper in this zone and refill the wells of this zone.

29. To compensate for depressed fire, it is necessary to follow *bhasrika pranayam*, drink gold soup every morning and take *ashvagandha*, an ayurvedic herb. This remedy is applicable to males staying in the house. Along with Vaastu rectification, it is necessary to treat the occupants with such remedies.

30. Disturbed vibration of South-East zone has malefic effects on the young growing sons in the house. Road hitting or well in this zone leads to the loss of son by fire hazard. A cosmic shield of 8-lined rudraksha, *Mahamrutyunjay* jap and fast on *Pradosh* are necessary to avoid such an event.

31. Kitchen in the South-East zone with gas stove in the *nabha* division leads to a balanced Fire element. In *Nabha* division, food attains a divine dimension due to the cosmic power of Akash tatwa. Ninety

percent population being non-vegetarian, this intense zone is suggested for kitchen. Meat from sacrificed animals (*bali*) is equated with South-East zone.

32. Toilets, well, road hitting, depression and terrace in this zone are *mahadosh*, i.e. severe faults in this zone. If not rectified then they result in severe damage to the occupants of the house. Bury copper in this zone, do copper panelling on doors and walls, use yellow colour flooring and provide pyramidal roof to regulate the vibration of this zone.

33. If South zone has a stable Earth element, it gives virtuous dimension to the organic streams of North. South zone represents high thermal and radiation zone, so if it is not properly loaded with the Earth element then the whole Vaastu gets disturbed and ruined. It is the first hypersensitive zone in Vaastu and needs serious focus while Vaastu analysis.

34. South is the sink direction of bio-magnetism i.e. *jaivik urja*. Only a strong expression of the Earth element can absorb the poison of South, and may regulate the energy pattern.

35. An Audumbar plant with stone platform and Jaisalmer yellow tile cladding around it establishes the Earth element in South. This plant has a stable bio-rhythm to absorb all the negativities of zone. It is considered as the highest divine element.

36. Due to the attributes of Earth element, this zone is marked for master bedroom, toilets, staircase, godowns and storerooms. On the magnetic axis, head in the South while sleeping is a highly appreciated position. To understand the importance of this direction, South is marked on top and North is marked down in Feng Shui.

37. South zone is governed by Saturn and Mars. Saturn rules under the ground and Mars rules on the entire

sky of the South zone. Hence, South is sandwiched between two strong enemy planets and needs careful attention during Vaastu analysis. In astrology, a natural horoscope shows a strong Earth element in the sign 'Capricorn' where Saturn is in its own house and Mars is in exalted position.

38. Roof slope and ground slope towards South, road hitting from South, terraces and large site margins in South, and depressions, borewells, septic tanks in South are considered severe faults. It is beneficial to discard such houses and search for a new one.

39. Yellow flooring, pyramidal roofs, heavy plantation, lead metal under flooring, copper panelling on doors and walls, stone cladding and raised flooring adds a virtuous expression of Earth element. This absorbs all negativities and cosmic irregularities. If all the above remedies are critically followed in the South zone, there is no fear of deity Yama.

40. Houses which have experienced loss of father (male in the age range of thirty to fifty) suffer from the above-mentioned faults related to South. Hence, cosmic shield of 8-line rudraksha, chanting of Mahamrutyunjay japa, regular follow-up of *Sudarshan kriya* is mandatory in such houses. All the measures mentioned above to stabilise the Earth element are absolutely necessary in the house.

41. South-West represents a strong Earth element where the virtues of Earth support seeding, reproduction and regeneration. Hence, newly married couples and males below the age of fifty should have this zone for bedroom. In traditional language this is called *shringarshala*, i.e. the place of romance. Hence, first priority to newly married couples and then others.

42. South-West is the zone of planet Rahu, which is the severe poison – unpredictable, cruel – and fire.

To absorb all these vices, a strong Earth element is required. If we observe the posture of *Vaastu purush* then it is obvious that this is the zone of *apana*, i.e. discharge, and legs in this zone indicate support and balance. Hence, fault in SW zone disturbs the balance and support of the house.

43. This zone connects West and South, where both represent sink of *prana*, i.e. sink of organic streams. Hence, this is the main sink direction. If there is fault in this direction then sinking in every aspect is experienced by the occupants. A strong and virtuous Earth element can annihilate the sinking character of this direction.

44. Roof slope and ground slope towards South-West, septic tank, underground water tank and borewell in South-West, extention and cut in South-West, road hitting from the South-West are considered *mahadosh*, i.e. severe faults. All faults of this direction have a malefic effect on the *grihaswami*, i.e. owner of the house. The above faults lead to death, destruction, demolition and defamation.

45. The 4 inner squares near Brahma in the South-West zone are reserved for the master bedroom. The deities here are Indra-Indrajay who represent royal sensuous happiness and success. Ever-expanding ambition and alertness are two important virtues of deity Indra with which the *grihaswami*, i.e. owner of the house, is blessed.

46. In natural horoscope, this zone represents the eight and ninth houses, i.e. death and fortune. Hence, if vibration of this zone gets disturbed then it will lead to death. A powerful Earth element in the South-West gives definite luck. While analysing Vaastu, the expert should give first and foremost importance to this direction.

47. Pyramidal roof, stone cladding, christmas and almond trees, *Tulsi vrindavan*, heavy landscape, yellow colour flooring, crystal and yellow sapphires, master bedroom and lead metal are some important features of this direction to create a perfect balance of energy, and to create a right expression of the Earth element.

48. Place a lead pyramid of weight 50kg in SW zone of the house, reload this zone with 3-4 truckload of black stones in factory, raise this zone by 6" with use of wooden or Jaisalmer yellow stone in the office, to change the energy-matter equation of Vaastu and produce miraculous results.

49. Wind as a 'storm' is the element of West. Hence, it is wise to create a situation in the house such that this 'storm' does not enter at all. Once the storm enters the house, a devastating loss is certain to happen. 'Control the West' is the second important sermon of Vaastushastra.

50. Sun and Moon both set in the West. In a way, this direction represents the sinking of mind and self. In Jainism, this direction is explained as *'Padmant'* direction, where lotus shrinks and contracts. In Feng Shui, West means disagreement in every walk of life. Subatomic particles, which can cause malignant effects in the body, are found in a huge number in this direction. West is the sink direction of *pranik* energy and hence needs serious care.

51. In natural horoscope, West represents the sign Libra, which represents Vayu tatwa. Its ruling planet is Venus with Saturn in ascendant. Venus, Saturn and Mercury are fast friends and all the three enjoy celebration in this direction. If this direction is not disturbed then one enjoys the royalty of Venus, the verdict of Saturn and the right decision of Mercury.

52. Pyramidal roof in aluminum foil, raised floors in blue-silver colour, metal articles, stainless steel, brass panelling on doors, peepal tree or bonsai that does not cast shadow on the house, no extensions and cuts, no depressions and water bodies, blue-film on the window glass, less site margin are some important additions to stabilise the storm of West and to enjoy the cool evening breeze in life.

53. Terraces, balconies, roof and ground slopes, cuts extensions, and a lot of light from this direction excite these sinking western streams, leading to disagreement in relation to family, wife and partners. Very often, this situation leads to defeat in court matters and partnerships. Severe multiple faults joining hands with South-East zone may lead to violence and jail.

54. One mystical remedy for the faults of West is to keep a blue bottle filled with edible oil and 7 nails in the West zone. Hide this bottle in the West zone on a Saturday morning. Any problems related to land, court and relationships may find an immediate solution. Blue represents the Wind element, oil represents Saturn, and nails are used to pierce the negative spirits. An assembly of all three in perfect sequence in the West zone may give a magical experience.

55. Traditionally, West zone is called *rangashala* signifying a ruling of Venus, Mercury and the Wind element. Art, luxury, humour, romance, magic, appreciation, music and drama of life finds root in this zone and if this zone is controlled then life becomes a celebration of a variety of experiences.

56. Placing 1 blue sapphire under the flooring nearer the Brahma in '*Mitra*' division controls the West zone, adds grace to the Wind element, contracts the

negative energy, and establishes the positive bliss of deity Varun.

57. NW zone is reserved for unmarried daughters in the house. Particularly, the 4 divisions near Brahma, named as Rudra, Rudrajay deities are used for the bedroom. This zone represents wind as harmony and moon as light. If daughter's bedroom is in this zone then she attains the rhythm of harmony and moon's delight.

58. To control the ever-changing moods and currents of wind, and to limit the high-low moods of moon, blue sapphire, a stone of Saturn, is used in this zone. It is buried particularly in the division near Brahma. Saturn represents patience, a long site and a practical guide. Such a hard master can do wonders for this zone of Moon and Wind.

59. This zone represents the positive side of Wind element called *svar, prana*, harmony and rhythm of music. Enhancing this zone removes friction from life and adds colours to the concert of life. Blue and silver colours, wind chimes, old traditional musical instruments, antique metal articles, brass and stainless steel panelling on doors and walls, blue-silver glass hundi on the ceiling, lots of light are some positive features of this zone.

60. This being a streaming source zone, bedroom of young couples in this zone can lead to repetitive abortions as conception is denied in this zone. A change of bedroom can give positive effect to young couples. That is how it gets proved that in Vaastu zones, activity of life and breath have a deep relation.

61. If kitchen is placed in this zone then the North-West zone gets blocked due to the heavy load of kitchen platform, fridge, oven and trollies. Kitchen represents sacrifice because of the presence of non-

veg food items. It also represents a strong fire which disturbs the elements of this zone. Non-veg food disturbs the sanctity of the zone and load blocks the positive stream.

62. This zone is associated with unmarried daughters who represent the prestige, ethics and grace of the family. Kitchen in this zone disqualifies the positivity of this zone, leading to late marriages of daughters, and gossip in society regarding their characters, leading to a loss of esteem of the family.

63. Extentions, cuts, load, raised zones, blockage, road hitting, kitchen and terraces are some severe faults associated with this direction. Being a positive and passive zone, faults in this zone do not create panic in life unless these faults join hands with other directions, particularly of the South-East zone.

64. Astrologically, this zone represents the fifth and sixth house, which represent the aspirations of sex, education, children, enemy, disease and accidents. A kitchen in this zone is a fault but kitchen not lying in the South-East zone is an additional fault since these directions are complementary (lie on 180 axis). Wind and Fire being the elements of these directions, it may lead to allergies, blood pressure and paralysis to the owner of the house.

65. Energy streaming and zones are the two aspects of Vaastu analysis. Flats with entry from the North and bedrooms in the South have correct sleeping zones. Normally, the direction of light is opposite to the entrance, so entry from the North leads to a lot of light from the South. Flats with entry from the West have bedrooms in the East zone, which is wrong but a lot of light comes from the East, which is good. Hence, in flats you get either correct streaming or a correct zone, but it is difficult to satisfy both the aspects.

66. A seed thrown in water gets degenerated, a seed thrown in wind gets carried away, a seed thrown in fire gets burnt. Only seeds thrown in earth may lead to germination, then a plant, a tree, a flower and ultimately the fruit and shade. Hence, the basis of eventology is the Earth element and Vaastu is a science of the Earth element.

67. A construction with C-shaped opening towards North is called 'som-choola' which assures fulfillment of all wishes. Such a place is a wish pond that gives peace, prosperity and progress. This means a cut is allowed in the North direction. In modern architecture, ducts, terraces and voids in the North equate to som-choola.

68. A construction with C-shaped opening towards East is called 'aaditya-choola' which assures power, courage, education and light in life. Hence, educational, academic and institutional buildings should prefer this shape. East is called as 'mohanta', i.e. end of greed and lust. So government buildings should prefer this shape to reduce corruption.

69. North contains mind, East contains intelligence and the confluence direction North-East contains the divine spirit that unifies mind and intellect. Hence, houses with North, North-East and East streams lead to harmony, bliss and grace. Every moment becomes a celebration in such a house.

70. The ideal house has a C-cut form towards East on the ground floor, C-cut form towards North on the first floor and L-shaped form opening out to North-East on the second floor. In such a house, energy streams move in a mandalakar form effortlessly, leading to the flowering of aspirations of all directions.

Ground floor
Poorva Choola

First Floor
Uttar Choola

Second Floor
Ishanya Dvi-shala

71. Skylight is a vertical light, which when falls on the floor, energises the deity of that zone. To stabilise the North, North-East and East deities, i.e. Som, Isha and Aditya in the house, a simple trick is to make holes in the ceiling to fetch skylight, a hole in the core of the slab. Bliss of Som leads to expansion of mind. Grace of Isha leads to fulfillment of purpose. Light of Aaditya leads to correct decision.

72. '*Viprit agni*' means disturbed Fire element, that is, faults in the East and South-East zone. Fire represents hunger, thirst and desire when it is disturbed. All criminals have *viprit agni* in their house and horoscopes. Normally, all such people have Saturn and Rahu in Aries, Leo and Sagittarius signs, i.e. 1, 5 and 9 in their horoscopes. All such criminals have either cuts or extensions in the South-East zone.

73. *Viprit agni* means fire getting depressed, that is Water element in the East and South-East zones. In such cases, fire represents loss of power, disturbed male hormones and no child condition. To stabilise Fire, a regular exercise of *kapalbhati*, use of ayurvedic herbs like *ashvagandha*, and drinking gold soup is a must for the young males staying in the house, along with Vaastu rectification.

74. *Viprit agni* means Fire element in the zone of other elements. In such cases, this fire burns the aspiration of that zone. This means if kitchen is in the West zone, this leads to tensions in the marital relationship. If kitchen is in the North-West zone, it results in problems related to the character of daughters or delaying of their marriages. If kitchen is in the North zone then it disturbs the health of the mother, etc.

75. Toilets, well, water tank, extensions and cuts, depression, septic tank in the East and South-East

zone lead to *viprit agni*. This results in negativity among the occupants of the house.

76. Positive energy travels in a clockwise, helical path (*pradakshina marg*) whereas negative energy ascends in fragmented loops in anticlockwise pattern or in intense straight-hitting pattern. Hence, faults in Vaastu create energy loops in anticlockwise pattern - *heen bahu*. If there is a borewell in the South zone then its disturbance will reach the house from the South-East or the East zone. If there is depression in the West then its ascending negative energy will attack the house from the South-West zone by moving in anticlockwise direction.

77. North, North-East and North-West represent moon stream, *chandra ida nadi*, Water element and ladies in the house. Any fault in these directions will reflect on the ladies staying in the house. This being a passive zone (yin), effects take place slowly, passively, like a slow poison.

78. South-East, South and South-West represent sun streams, *surya pingala nadi*, active energy and males staying in the house. Any fault in this set of directions reflects on the males staying in the house. This being an active zone, effects happen suddenly, intensely, like accidental death, suicide or murder.

79. The sole purpose of this science is to create a positive confluence of personal and cosmic breath and to reduce blockage, friction and impediments. This correct relationship with nature gives rhythm, synchronicity and frequency, leading to the rejuvenation of the aura which acts as a cosmic shield against premature death and all types of diseases. Traditionally, this is explained as *"Akal Mrutyharanam, Sarva Yadhivinashanam"* (अकाल मृत्युहरणं, सर्व व्याधीविनाशनं)

80. *Vaastu-Nabhi* is the dynamic centre of the Vaastu. Ascending helical streaming of cosmic energy finds its epicenter in this point. The ritual of placement of *Nabhi-Shanku* assures bliss, grace and light by realigning the elements in the right zone, forcing energy to travel in a *pranavakar–mandalakar* way and by re-establishing the deities in the correct zone.

81. If the proportion of openings in a house are in the ratio of 4:3:2:1 with reference to N:E:W:S then automatically energy travels in a *mandalakar* helical path. This leads to the flowering of aspirations of all zones. All the deities get a bliss of positive energy and in turn they contribute bliss, grace and peace to the occupants. 4 windows in North, 3 windows in East, 2 windows in West and 1 window in South is a divine proportion to attain health and happiness.

82. In modern flat system, some flats have good energy streaming from North and East, but zones of sleeping and cooking may not match. Some flats have correct zones of sleeping and cooking but energy streaming is from South and West. Hence, in modern flat system, every flat needs a Vaastu treatment either for energy correction or for zone-rectification.

83. When Saturn or Rahu enters the fire signs Aries, Leo or Sagittarius then the cosmic East gets polluted, and cosmic Fire gets disturbed. This affects all houses which have faults on the East-West axis. So during this period, people staying in houses with toilets in East, East closed, C-cut towards West, roof slope or ground slope towards West should take care by correcting the East-West axis in their house.

84. When Saturn or Rahu enters the water signs Cancer, Scorpio or Pisces then the cosmic North gets polluted and cosmic Water gets disturbed. This affects all houses which have fault on the North-South axis. So during this period, people staying in houses with

toilets in North, North closed, terrace facing South, staircase in North, C-cut towards South, roof slope and ground slope towards South should take care by correcting the North-South axis in their house.

85. Contribution of positive energy is slow, passive and disciplined. It is like a seed growing into a plant, plant becoming a tree, tree producing flowers and ultimately, if everything goes well, getting the fruit. But negative energy can wipe out this whole organic movement in just one stroke. Hence, the first and foremost duty of a Vaastu expert is to control negativity, i.e. South, South-West and West and then to enhance positivity, i.e. North, North-East and East aspirations.

86. A correct relationship with light leads to emergence of life, intelligence and flowering whereas an incorrect relationship with light leads to the expression of death, bad events and voids. Vaastu is a magical art that acts as an organic enclave to regulate the travel of light and energy in *mandalakar* way, leading to divine experience, blissful moments and graceful movement. In traditional language it is said *"Gati Twam Gati Twam, Twame Ka bhavani"* (गतिस्त्वम्। गतिस्त्वम्। त्वकेका भवानी)

87. *Vaastu-Nabhi* is the dynamic centre of Vaastu around which energy gets expressed in the *mandalakar,* helical, *pranavakar* way. In case of faults in the Vaastu, this dynamic centre shifts, leading to multiple anticlockwise loops of negative energy. These anticlockwise loops of energy get absorbed by the Earth element, if it is placed in a particular discipline in the house. Vaastu analysis calls for an energy-matter equation which needs to be solved in a dynamic way.

88. Correction of the East-West axis includes a) burying copper in East zone; b) burying red coral in East zone

c) copper panelling on doors of East and South-East zone; d) creating skylight in the East zone; e) using white marble flooring in the East zone; f) keeping banyan bonsai in East zone; g) burying lead/brass in West zone; h) providing pyramidal ceiling in metallic foil in West zone; i) keeping a peepal bonsai in West zone; j) using blue tile flooring in West zone; k) burying 7 steel rods in West site margin; l) loading the West zone; m) providing *shanitarka yantra* on the West wall; n) using blue glass for West windows; o) burying blue Sapphire in West zone.

89. Surroundings dictate the form of Vaastu and house (*Ghat-Bimb Siddhant*). Quality of Sky depends on the container and accordingly, virtues of the contents dictate the order of life. So the form of house plays the most important role in deciding the future of a human being. An intelligent Vaastu expert never gets victimised by the stroke of surroundings while planning the house. Whatever the outer form of energy be, once it starts moving in a *mandalakar* way, it always leads to quality, virtue and positivity.

90. *Viprit jal* means excessive water or water in the wrong zone or polluted water. Excessive water in house leads to female progeny and issueless conditions. Water in the wrong zone disturbs the aspirations of that direction, e.g. water in East and South-East reduces the power of Fire element, leading to multiple faults like no-child condition, loss of son and accidents; water in West and North-West excites the Wind element, leading to immorality and vices; water in South and South-West zones disturbs the Earth element, leading to instability, accidents and suicides. If toilets are in North/North-East zone then it pollutes the Water element, leading to serious health problems for the ladies staying in the house.

91. Sky is the most powerful element. Sky contains the clouds of events and winds of possibilities. If Sky is disturbed then events and possibilities do not find a proper space in life, leading to a chaotic condition. Houses with C-cut towards South and West and ducts in South-East and South-West zones lead to *viprit antaral,* i.e. wrong sky. Roof slopes towards South and West lead to disturbance in the house due to hyper thermal projection of the roof. This leads to thermal torque and high radiation. This is also called *viprit antral* (wrong sky).

92. North light roof leads to main roof slope towards South, in a way, projecting the entire roof surface to the scorching sun. This creates disturbance in the bio-magnetic field, leading to many anticlockwise fragmented loops of cosmic energy. As a result, Sky virtue gets disturbed, leading to loss of clouds of events and winds of possibilities. All such industrial structures lead to failure, lockouts and liquidation.

93. Surrounding of your house is the extension of the aspirations, faults and virtues of the zone. If a zone is faulty then one can find that imbalance in the surroundings expressed by some symbol. This symbol is called the flag of the *Vikshep devta* (deity of the outer perimeter), that creates disturbance. A wise Vaastu expert can predict the eventology of the house just by observing the surroundings and flags, without entering the house.

94. Esoteric Vaastu is the art of reading eventology attached to a house by observing the symbols, symptoms and surroundings related to the house. Esoteric Vaastu is the combination of Yang Vaastu and Yin Vaastu, so one can read the past of bad events in connection with one's forefathers. Spaces are of Sun and Moon. Darkness of voids contains clouds of past consciousness. Esoteric Vaastu is the

divine art that can erase the past and help in the flowering of future.

95. Sky creates events, Light and Water regulate those events, Fire energises these events and Wind creates the movement of *prana* in the events. Earth holds the events to propagate them at the right time in the life of the occupants. Irregularity in the nature of any of these elements creates asymmetry and wrong placement, leading to unsatisfaction and incompleteness in life.

96. Bits of quanta and moments of time contain the divine code of information. Rhythm of energy, balancing of elements and power of direction decode this mystical code to write the poetry of life, like threads are woven step by step to create the colourful fabric of human life. When the order of energy disappears then discipline in life gets subtracted and life becomes chaotic. It is the dynamic matrix of nature, order and discipline / rhythm, integrity and vitality / peace, prosperity and progress.

97. Macrocosm contains the intense unbound and profound power. It contains the megascale of Fire, Wind, Water and Earth, which cannot possibly be correlated with limited human existence. Microcosm contains the subtle, well-bound and delicate forms of power. It contains the miniscale (*sookshma*) representation of Fire as ego, Wind as intelligence, Water as mind and Earth as body. Vaastu is a medium that regulates the immensity of macrocosm to formulate the digestible, palatable form which works as the extension of human existence.

98. Vaastu is a living organic experience which shares happiness if it is healthy, and sorrow, if it is diseased. It is a gathering of 81 deities, 8 directions, 5 great elements, 9 planets and the human being. If all the entities are tuned properly then it leads

to a wonderful concert, and if any of them is in discord then life becomes full of confusion, chaos and calamity.

99. Fire is expressed in four forms. It is smoke when depressed. It is flame when exalted. It is warmth when controlled, and it is radiant when it is very close. Fire with Earth leads to warmth and gives a pleasing effect. Hence, Fire in South-East is controlled by regulating the Earth element.

100. Measures to correct North-South axis:
   a) bury silver and pearls in the North zone
   b) make depression in the North zone
   c) provide windows and roof slope towards North
   d) create skylight in the North zone
   e) keep a water body/fountain with crystal white marble, pearls and mirror in the North zone
   f) if North zone is faulty then take care of the health of ladies in the house
   g) remove toilets, loads and staircase from the North zone
   h) make an additional borewell in the North zone
   i) use yellow glass for southern windows
   j) bury lead in South zone
   k) encase 9 lead rods in the South wall
   l) do not make any well or boring or underground watertank in the South zone
   m) 1 audumbar tree with stone platform and yellow stone cladding does wonders in the South zone
   n) paint southern roof slopes in yellow and provide pyramidal roof to spaces inside the house
   o) provide 9 golden flags or 9 mounds in landscaping or 9 christmas trees in South zone.
   p) keep the least site margin in South zone, so that the load of the house falls in the South zone.

Glossary

Bhasrika	:	It is breathing technique that leads to fire in body.
Dik-kal	:	Dik means direction and Kal means time. Dikkal is a term used to explain the interdependence of direction and time.
Ida-Chandra Nadi	:	These are positive currents of cosmic energy and individual breath.
Jaivik Urja	:	These are organic energy streams which control all bio-chemical formulations in the world.
Kal-Purush-Kundali	:	This is a natural horoscope with Aries as the ascendant.
Mantra beej	:	Primordial sound.
Mukti	:	Liberation
Pingala or surya nadi	:	These are negative currents of cosmic energy and individual breath.
Poornima Siddhant	:	When the sun is on Western horizon, and the moon is relatively on Eastern horizon, then moon exhibits full moon effect, or the principle of Poornima Siddhant.
Pranik energy	:	Solar streams are the carrier of this energy. This energy is the main stream of energy on which all activities in nature are dependent.
Rudraksha	:	It is a divine fruit from the Himalayas.
Suvarna Jal	:	It is a water therapy with effect of gold.
Sudarshan Kriya	:	Rhythmic dynamic breathing technique founded by H H Sri Sri Ravishankar.
Tirthankar	:	Enlightened souls.
Trishala-Dovishala	:	Set of 3 and 2 houses.
Yogadhipati	:	Every horoscope has a planet which is beneficial to it called Yogadhipati.

143